Level
3

Read and Succeed:
Comprehension

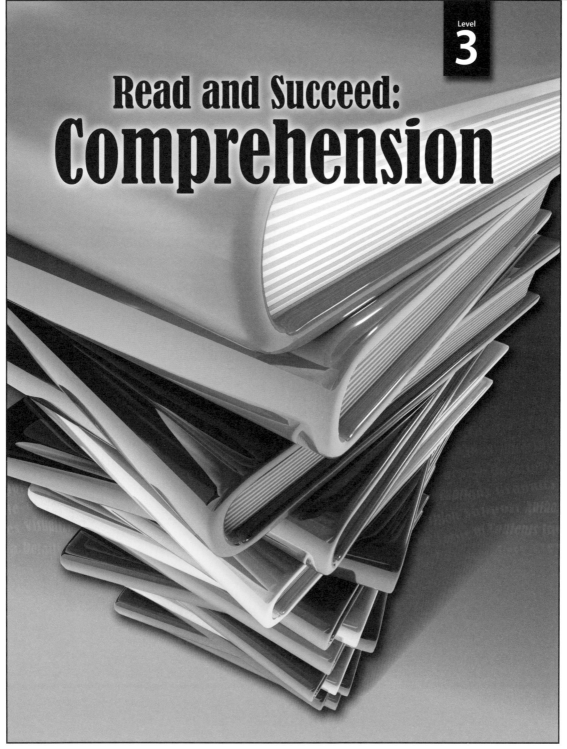

Consultant

Debra J. Housel, M.S.Ed.

SHELL EDUCATION

Contributing Authors

Sharon Coan

Jennifer Kroll

Kathleen C. Petersen

Publishing Credits

Dona Herweck Rice, *Editor-in-Chief*; Lee Aucoin, *Creative Director*; Don Tran, *Print Production Manager;* Timothy J. Bradley, *Illustration Manager*; Conni Medina, M.A.Ed., *Editorial Director*; Kristy Stark, M.A.Ed., *Editor*; Stephanie Reid, *Cover Designer;* Robin Erickson, *Interior Layout Designer;* Corinne Burton, M.S.Ed., *Publisher*

Copyright 2004 McRel. www.mcrel.org/standards-benchmarks.

Shell Education

5301 Oceanus Drive
Huntington Beach, CA 92649-1030
http://www.shelleducation.com
ISBN 978-1-4258-0726-9
©2010 Shell Educational Publishing, Inc.
Reprinted 2013

The classroom teacher may reproduce copies of materials in this book for classroom use only. The reproduction of any part for an entire school or school system is strictly prohibited. No part of this publication may be transmitted, stored, or recorded in any form without written permission from the publisher.

Table of Contents

Introduction

Comprehension is the goal of every reading task. The *Read and Succeed: Comprehension* series can help lay the foundation of comprehension skills that are essential for a lifetime of learning. The series was written specifically to provide the purposeful practice students need in order to succeed in reading comprehension. The more students practice, the more confident and capable they can become.

Why You Need This Book

- **It is standards based**. The skill practice pages are aligned to the Mid-continent Research for Education and Learning (McREL) standards. (See page 7.)
- **It has focused lessons**. Each practice page covers a key comprehension skill. Skills are addressed multiple times to provide several opportunities for mastery.
- **It employs advanced organization**. Having students encounter the question page first gives them a "heads up" when they approach the text, thereby enhancing comprehension and promoting critical-thinking abilities.
- **It has appropriate reading levels**. All passages have a grade level calculated based on the Shell Education leveling system, which was developed under the guidance of Dr. Timothy Rasinski, along with the staff at Shell Education.
- **It has an interactive whiteboard-compatible Teacher Resource CD.** This can be used to enhance instruction and support literacy skills.

How to Use This Book

First, determine what sequence will best benefit your students. Work through the book in order (as the skills become progressively more difficult) to cover all key skills. For reinforcement of specific skills, select skills as needed.

Then determine what instructional setting you will use. See below for suggestions for a variety of instructional settings:

Whole-Class or Small-Group Instruction	Independent Practice or Centers	Homework
Read and discuss the Skill Focus. Write the name of the skill on the board.	Create a folder for each student. Include a copy of the selected skill practice page and passage.	Give each student a copy of the selected skill practice page and passage.
Read and discuss responses to each question. Read the text when directed (as a group, in pairs, or individually).	Have students complete the skill practice page. Remind them to begin by reading the Skill Focus and to read the passage when directed.	Have students complete the skill practice page. Remind them to begin by reading the Skill Focus and to read the passage when directed.
Read and discuss the Critical Thinking question. Allow time for discussion before having students write their responses.	Collect the skill practice pages and check students' answers. Or, provide each student with a copy of the answer key (pages 138–149).	Collect the skill practice pages and check students' answers. Or, provide each student with a copy of the answer key (pages 138–149).

Research Support for the
Read and Succeed: Comprehension Series

Comprehension is the ability to derive meaning from text. It is critically important not only for the development of children's reading skills but also for students' abilities to obtain a complete education. The National Reading Panel (2000) states that comprehension is an active process that requires an intentional interaction between the reader and the text. A reader must engage in problem-solving thinking processes in order to relate the ideas represented in print to his or her own knowledge and experiences and build mental images to store in memory.

Teaching students to use specific strategies can improve their comprehension. To some degree, readers acquire such strategies informally. However, the National Reading Panel confirmed that explicit instruction in comprehension strategies is highly effective in enhancing understanding. That's why the *Read and Succeed: Comprehension* series was created: to make teaching comprehension strategies simple and time efficient. This book teaches specific strategies students can use to help them understand what they are reading.

Having students know in advance the questions they will be asked helps them to attend to the material. It gives them a focus as they read. It helps them to look for clues and to identify information they will need to remember. But most importantly, it allows them to organize information in their minds, building neural pathways that will be used again and again. Essentially, having a focus as they read teaches children how to think. This is why the skill practice page always appears before the reading passage in *Read and Succeed: Comprehension.*

Teaching a combination of reading comprehension techniques is the most effective approach for instruction. When students use strategies appropriately, they can improve their recall, question answering, question generation, and summarization of texts. Also, used in combination, these techniques can improve results in standardized comprehension tests. Yet teaching reading comprehension strategies to students at all grade levels can be complex. The *Read and Succeed: Comprehension* series was designed to make this process straightforward. Each book contains 65 lessons. Each lesson has a specific focus to concentrate on an important reading skill for a fiction or a nonfiction text. Step by step, students will learn the grade-level-appropriate skills they need to read and understand a wide variety of texts.

Each skill activity is independent; they need not be done in a certain order. However, it is in students' best interest to complete all of the activities. Using the *Read and Succeed: Comprehension* series will save you time and effort while simultaneously providing students with the vital skills needed to achieve 21st century comprehension and critical-thinking skills.

National Institute of Child Health and Human Development. 2000. *Report of the National Reading Panel. Teaching children to read: An evidence-based assessment of the scientific research literature on reading and its implications for reading instruction* (NIH Publication No. 00-4769). Washington, DC: U.S. Government Printing Office.

Standards Correlations

Shell Education is committed to producing educational materials that are research and standards based. In this effort, we have correlated all of our products to the academic standards of all 50 states, the District of Columbia, and the Department of Defense Dependent Schools.

How to Find Standards Correlations

To print a customized correlation report of this product for your state, visit our website at **www.shelleducation.com** and follow the on-screen directions. If you require assistance in printing correlation reports, please contact Customer Service at 1-877-777-3450.

Purpose and Intent of Standards

The No Child Left Behind legislation mandates that all states adopt academic standards that identify the skills students will learn in kindergarten through grade twelve. While many states had already adopted academic standards prior to NCLB, the legislation set requirements to ensure the standards were detailed and comprehensive.

Standards are designed to focus instruction and guide adoption of curricula. Standards are statements that describe the criteria necessary for students to meet specific academic goals. They define the knowledge, skills, and content students should acquire at each level. Standards are also used to develop standardized tests to evaluate students' academic progress.

Teachers are required to demonstrate how their lessons meet state standards. State standards are used in development of all of our products, so educators can be assured they meet the academic requirements of each state.

McREL Compendium

We use the Mid-continent Research for Education and Learning (McREL) Compendium to create standards correlations. Each year, McREL analyzes state standards and revises the compendium. By following this procedure, McREL is able to produce a general compilation of national standards. Each lesson in this product is based on one or more McREL standards. The chart on the following page lists each standard taught in this product and the page numbers for the corresponding lessons.

McREL Correlations Chart

Skills	Skill Focus and Page Numbers
Previews text	*Preview,* 8–9, 10–11
Establishes a purpose for reading	*Set a Purpose,* 20–21, 22–23; *Ask Questions,* 24–25, 26–27
Makes, confirms, and revises predictions	*Predict,* 12–13, 14–15; *Visualize,* 36–37, 38–39
Uses a variety of context clues to decode unknown words	*Context Clues,* 32–33, 34–35
Uses word reference materials (e.g., glossary) to determine the meaning, pronunciation, and derivations of unknown words	*Glossary,* 134–135, 136–137
Understands author's purpose or point of view	*Author's Purpose,* 94–95, 96–97
Uses reading skills and strategies to understand and interpret literary texts	*Story Elements,* 40–41, 42–43
Understands the basic concept of plot	*Plot,* 44–45, 46–47
Understands elements of character development	*Characters,* 48–49, 50–51
Makes connections between characters or events in a literary work and people or events in his or her own life	*Make Connections,* 28–29, 30–31
Uses reading skills and strategies to understand and interpret informational texts	*Fact and Opinion,* 86–87, 88–89; *Classify,* 102–103, 104–105; *Draw Conclusions,* 110–111, 112–113; *Infer,* 114–115, 116–117
Uses text organizers (e.g., headings, topic and summary sentences, graphic features, typeface, chapter titles) to determine the main ideas and to locate information in a text	*Topic Sentences,* 64–65, 66–67; *Title and Headings,* 52–53, 54–55; *Typeface and Captions,* 56–57, 58–59; *Graphics,* 60–61, 62–63
Identifies the main idea and supporting details	*Main Idea,* 68–69, 70–71; *Details,* 72–73, 74–75; *Main Idea and Details,* 76–77
Uses the various parts of a book to locate information (e.g., table of contents, index)	*Table of Contents,* 126–127, 128–129; *Index,* 130–131, 132–133
Summarizes and paraphrases information in texts	*Summarize,* 118–119, 120–121; *Paraphrase,* 122–123, 124–125
Uses prior knowledge and experience to understand and respond to new information	*Prior Knowledge,* 16–17, 18–19
Understands structural patterns or organization in informational texts (e.g., chronological, logical, or sequential order; compare and contrast; cause and effect; proposition and support)	*Time Order,* 78–79, 80–81; *Logical Order,* 82–83, 84–85; *Compare and Contrast,* 98–99, 100–101; *Cause and Effect,* 106–107, 108–109; *Proposition and Support,* 90–91, 92–93

Preview

Skill Focus

Looking at the title, pictures, and headings before you read helps you to get ready to understand the text.

1. Preview the text. Skim the headings. Will this text be about fashion or how things are made? What makes you think so?

   _____

   _____

2. Below each heading, look for names with capital letters. Which two names are mentioned?

   _____

   _____

3. Read the text. Write two new facts that you learned about clothing.

   _____

   _____

Critical Thinking

If you needed to find the date that Levi Strauss created jeans, how do the headings help you to find that fact quickly?

_____

_____

_____

In Your Closet

You look in your closet and say, "Mom, I don't have a thing to wear! Can we go shopping?" You may spend hours in the store choosing garments. You want to wear clothes that make you look and feel good. But where do all those clothes in the store come from? Who made them, and how?

Jeans

If you're like most people your age, you have some jeans. Levi Strauss invented them for gold miners in 1873. Today's jeans look much like the first ones. The pockets still have copper rivets. Strauss added them to make the pockets strong so that miners could carry gold nuggets.

Raincoats

If you own a raincoat, you can thank Charles Macintosh. He made the first waterproof cloth. He put a thin rubber coating on two pieces of cloth. He pressed the pieces together with the rubber in between. The rubber stuck together. He used this cloth to make raincoats. People bought them because they could stay dry when it rained.

Shoes

Years ago, cobblers made shoes for people when they ordered them. After they measured the person's foot, they chose the shoe form that best matched. The cobblers used the form to cut leather uppers and soles. They sewed together the pieces of the uppers. Finally, they used tiny wooden pegs to attach the uppers and soles. All of this took days. Today, shoe pieces are cut and put together on machines. Some shoes are stitched, and others are glued. This makes shoes cost less, so people can afford more pairs.

A shoe assembly line

Preview

Looking at the title, pictures, and headings before you read helps you to get ready to understand the text.

1. Preview the text. Write what you think the text will be about.

    _____

    _____

2. Skim the bulleted information. Look for the words with capital letters. Which two nations are mentioned?

    _____   _____

3. Read the text. The author says that the Space Station is "like" something you will recognize. What is it, and why did the author use that comparison?

    _____

    _____

    _____

Critical Thinking

Why are the events in the Space Station history section listed in the order in which they occurred?

_____

_____

_____

The International Space Station

There are many exciting things in space. But the International Space Station is amazing. It is the largest object in space made by people. It is like a small city floating in space.

People can live on the space station. The first crew went there in 2000. Sixteen countries work together there. Each one hopes to learn more about space.

This space "city" is big. And it is still growing. When it is done, it will be longer than a football field. Yet the International Space Station is not the first space station.

Space Station History

- People thought of building a space station long ago. The first idea was in the United States in 1869. It was in a science fiction book.

- The Soviet Union made the first space station. It launched in 1971. It was called *Salyut 1*. The first crew landed there a few days later. The crew could not get the hatch open! They had to go back home.

- A second Soviet crew went to *Salyut 1*. They spent 22 days on board. Sadly, they died on the way home. Air had leaked out of their capsule.

- The first U.S. space station was called *Skylab*. *Skylab* went into orbit in 1973. Three crews lived on it from then until February 1974. *Skylab* fell to Earth five years later. It landed on a cow in Australia.

- Russia made the *Mir* space station. The first part of *Mir* launched in 1986. People lived on it for most of its time in space. *Mir* was brought back to Earth in March 2001. It crashed into the South Pacific Ocean.

Predict

Always look at the title and pictures before you read a text. Try to guess what the text will be about.

1. Read the beginning of the text and the first riddle. Solve the first riddle.

    _____

    Write the clues that helped you to know the answer.

    _____

2. Read the second riddle. Solve it: _____

    Write the clues that helped you to know the answer.

    _____

3. Read the third riddle. Draw a picture of the solution to the third riddle.

Write a prediction about what Lito may do when he grows up.

_____

_____

_____

bat; monkey; flying squirrel

?Guess? What It Is

Lito writes a column for his school newspaper. He likes to write riddles. Riddles tell you facts about something. Then you have to guess what the riddle is telling about. The children in Lito's school love reading his riddles and guessing the answers.

Here are three of Lito's favorite riddles. See if you can guess the correct answers.

1. I am tiny and have a furry body. I have smooth wings and sharp claws. I sleep most of the day and only fly at night. I make a high, sharp sound to find my favorite food—insects. What am I?

2. I have a furry body and a long, furry tail. I fly from tree to tree, but I don't have wings. I eat and play all day and sleep at night. I make chattering sounds as I eat my favorite food—fruit. People stand and watch me play at the zoo. They think I am funny. What am I?

3. I have a furry body and a long, furry tail. I can fly from tree to tree, but I don't have wings. I eat and play all day and sleep at night. I also hibernate most of the winter. I make a clicking sound if there is danger. My favorite foods are nuts and seeds. What am I?

The answers to Lito's riddles are printed on another page in the newspaper. The readers can turn to that page to check their guesses to see if they are right.

Predict

Always look at the title and pictures before you read a text. Try to guess what the text will be about.

Answer the first two questions *before* you read the story.

1. Look at the title. What animals will be in the story?

   _____

2. Do you think the animals in the story will get along? Explain.

   _____

   _____

3. Read the story. What might have happened if Coyote refused to take Scorpion across the stream?

   _____

   _____

   _____

Critical Thinking

How did your predictions compare with what actually happened in the story?

_____

_____

_____

COYOTE
AND THE SCORPION

It was a hot day. Coyote was thirsty. He wanted a cool drink. He decided to go down to the stream. Once there, he saw a movement in the grass.

"Good day, Coyote," said Scorpion, using his best manners. Coyote backed away. He knew Scorpion's tail was dangerous. Just one sting, and Coyote would be dead!

"Coyote, please don't run away from me," Scorpion cried. "The water in the stream is deep, and I cannot swim. Won't you please give me a ride across the water on your strong back?"

"No!" said Coyote. "If I let you climb on my back, you will sting me with your tail, and I will die."

"Don't be silly," said Scorpion. "If I sting you while we are crossing the stream, we will both drown. Please get into the water, and I will crawl up your tail and onto your back."

Coyote believed him. So he let Scorpion climb up his tail and onto his back. Off he swam. Halfway across the stream, Scorpion stung Coyote with his tail.

"Why did you do that?" screamed Coyote. He started to sink.

"I'm a scorpion, and stinging is what we scorpions do," replied Scorpion. Then they both sank beneath the water and drowned.

Prior Knowledge

Whenever you read, you bring what you already know about the subject to the text. You use this prior knowledge to make sense of the new information you read.

1. Write two things that you already know about crayons.

   _____

   _____

2. Read the text. Write two facts that you learned about crayons from the text.

   _____

   _____

3. Write two questions that you still have about crayons.

   _____

   _____

Critical Thinking

How did what you already knew about crayons make understanding this text easier?

_____

_____

_____

Colorful Crayons

You probably have lots of crayons. You know what they smell like, you know how to peel the paper off, and you know how to use them to color things. But did you know how they got their start?

The first crayons were made from a mixture of oil and charcoal. Can you picture taking some cooking oil and some charcoal from the grill and drawing with that? These crayons were pretty messy, so wax was used instead of oil to make them work better.

Two cousins named Binney and Smith were making a special kind of chalk for writing on boxes. They were adding wax to the chalk. This made the chalk almost like the old crayons. But they were better. They found a way to make lots of the colorful crayons.

In 1903, the first box of crayons was sold. There were eight in the box. The first colors were yellow, black, violet, blue, red, brown, orange, and green. That box cost just five cents. That was over one hundred years ago. Since then, there have been boxes with as many as 120 crayons! Could you use that many crayons?

Prior Knowledge

Whenever you read, you bring what you already know about the subject to the text. You use this prior knowledge to make sense of the new information you read.

1. Write two things that you already know about vampires.

   _____

   _____

2. Read the text. What does the vampire mean when he says some of the classrooms remind him of his coffin?

   _____

   _____

3. What might the vampire like to see on the school lunch menu?

   _____

   _____

Critical Thinking

How did what you already knew about vampires make understanding this text easier?

_____

_____

_____

Interview with the Springside School Vampire

By Scott "the Scoop" Porter

Scott the Scoop: You are, as far as I know, the only vampire in our school. What's that like for you?

Vampire: I've got to say, it's not easy being a vampire at Springside School.

Scott the Scoop: It isn't? What's so tough about it?

Vampire: For one thing, the school uniform drives me crazy. They make me leave my cape in my locker every day. It's hard to look scary in a polo shirt and tan pants.

Scott the Scoop: Yes, I can see that. What else is difficult for you?

Vampire: The school day. And by that, I mean the fact that classes are during the day. We vampires need to sleep during the daytime. We don't deal very well with sunlight, you know.

Scott the Scoop: I've heard that about vampires. Don't you catch fire if the sun shines directly on you?

Vampire: Yes, that can actually happen. It's a good thing most of the classrooms in this building have hardly any windows. A couple of them actually remind me of my cozy coffin.

Scott the Scoop: What's your opinion on school lunches?

Vampire: I think school lunches are totally gross! There's never anything on the menu I want to eat. So you see, it's not my fault if I get hungry by afternoon.

Set a Purpose

Before you read, ask yourself a question about the text based on the pictures or the title. Then read to find the answer. Having a purpose will help you to get more out of what you read.

1. Look at the title and picture. Write a question that you hope the text will answer.

   _____

   _____

2. Read the story. Write two things that you learned about panthers.

   _____

   _____

3. If you were going to add information to this text, which animal would you write more about? Why?

   _____

   _____

Critical Thinking

Did the text answer the question that you wrote for #1? If not, how can you find the answer?

   _____

   _____

   _____

A Visit to the Zoo

"The panthers are pretty!" said Elena.

"Yes, but they are also scary," said Haley.

"Panthers belong to the cat family," said Leo. "The adults weigh more than 100 pounds."

"A panther would make a great pet," Elena said.

"No, it wouldn't," said Leo. "It is against the law to keep a wild animal as a pet."

"This is the best field trip we have ever taken," Juan said.

Elena agreed, "I think it is fun, too. The zoo has so many animals for us to see."

"There are two types of chimps at this zoo," Juan said. "I think they're the best animals here!"

"I like the reindeer," said Haley. "They live where it is very cold."

As they got on the bus to go back to school, the teacher said, "We learned a lot today. Tomorrow, we will write stories about the zoo."

Set a Purpose

Before you read, ask yourself a question about the text based on the pictures or the title. Then read to find the answer. Having a purpose will help you to get more out of what you read.

1. Look at the title and picture. Write a question that you hope the text will answer.

   _____

   _____

2. Read the text. Write two things that you learned about how playing video games can be helpful to you.

   _____

   _____

3. If you were going to add information to this text, which video game would you write about? Why?

   _____

   _____

Critical Thinking

How did setting a purpose help you to understand the text better?

_____

_____

_____

Games Worth Playing

You are really into your favorite video game. Bet you aren't thinking about what you are learning. It's just plain fun! Before you start playing, take a minute to think. Is this a game worth playing?

Wait a minute. Let's think about this to get the big picture. Does the game make you come up with a plan? Do you have to really think in order to figure out which moves to make? Hmm. Maybe you are using more of your brain than you think.

Action games, where you use a controller to move players, can also develop good eye-hand coordination. You can give your brain a workout because your hands and eyes have to work together.

Speaking of workouts—have you tried one of the games that require your whole body to activate the game? Not only are you learning, but you are exercising, too. Now that's really a game worth playing!

Ask Questions

Before you read, ask yourself, "What questions do I have about this topic? What do I hope to learn?" Then as you read, look for the answers.

1. Look at the title. What do you already know about this topic?

   _____

   _____

2. On the chart below, write two questions that you hope the text will answer.

Question	Answer

3. Read the text. Write the answers to your questions in the chart above.

Critical Thinking

If one of your questions was not answered, how can you find the answer?

_____

_____

_____

Earthquake!

Imagine that you are sitting at the table, eating your breakfast. Suddenly, the milk in your cereal bowl starts to shake. Then the table begins to shake, too. The floor beneath your feet is moving, too! What is happening? It is an earthquake!

What should you do? Take cover! Get under a table or desk. Or, stand in the nearest doorway. Stay away from windows because they might shatter. Most of all, stay calm. You will be all right. Earthquakes that you can feel are pretty rare. Most earthquakes are mild, with little shaking. Usually, everyone is all right, and things are fine, although some things may be broken. An earthquake is a normal thing to happen on Earth.

Just what causes an earthquake? An earthquake happens when rocks break and slip along a fault in the earth. Earthquakes happen all over the world. However, most occur on active fault lines. Earthquakes occur every day around the globe. Luckily, most are very small, and we cannot feel them.

We know this because there are scientists, called *seismologists*, who study earthquakes. These people have learned a lot about earthquakes. Even so, no one can prevent an earthquake.

Ask Questions

Before you read, ask yourself, "What questions do I have about this topic? What do I hope to learn?" Then as you read, look for the answers.

1. Look at the title. What do you already know about this topic?

    _____

    _____

2. On the chart below, write two questions that you hope the text will answer.

Question	Answer

3. Read the text. Write the answers to your questions in the chart above.

Critical Thinking

If one of your questions was not answered, how can you find the answer?

_____

_____

_____

The Anemone

In the sea, a little fish swims in and out of what looks like cooked spaghetti. A bigger fish wants to eat the small fish. The big fish swims into the "spaghetti" to catch the little fish. Zap! The big fish is stung and paralyzed. The "diner" has just become the dinner!

At first glance, sea anemones (uh-NEM-oh-neez) look like flowers or clumps of wavering jelly. But anemones are animals. They can be found in tide pools or in the ocean. Those that live in tropical waters are the most colorful. Some are very small. Others are about 5 feet (1.5 meters) wide. They're shaped like a tube. They can be long and slender or short and stout. In most species, a sucker holds them to a rock or other hard surface.

At one end of the tube shape is the anemone's mouth. The mouth is ringed by tentacles. Each tentacle has small barbs that hold poison. When a shrimp or fish touches one of them, it is stung. The poison paralyzes the fish. This means that the fish cannot move. It cannot swim away. The fish is then guided into the anemone's mouth.

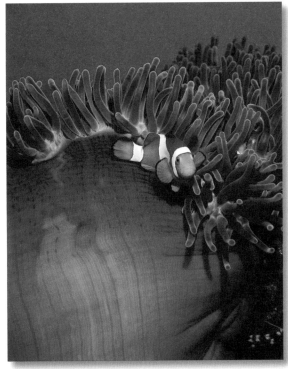

What about the little fish? Why doesn't it get stung? Actually, it does. But the anemone's poison does not bother the small fish—such as the clown fish—that hides within its tentacles.

A sea anemone with a clown fish

Make Connections

When you read, you use what you already know about the subject to understand the text. You use this prior knowledge to make sense of the new information you read.

1. Read the story. Is it true? How do you know?

   _____

   _____

2. Which fish are you most like? Explain.

   _____

   _____

3. Have you ever done something to help someone else? Explain.

   _____

   _____

4. What lesson did Thoughtful and Thoughtless learn?

   _____

   _____

Critical Thinking

When did you learn a lesson the hard way?

_____

_____

_____

© Shell Education

THE THREE FISHES

FROM MORE JATAKA TALES, RETOLD BY ELLEN C. BABBITT

Once upon a time, three fishes lived in a faraway river. Their names were Thoughtful, Very Thoughtful, and Thoughtless. One day, they left the wild country where no humans lived. They swam down the river to live near a town.

After just two days, Very Thoughtful said to the other two, "There is danger all around us. Fishermen come to the river here. They use nets and lines to catch fish. Let us return to the wild country."

But the other two fish were lazy. They kept putting off leaving each day.

One day, Thoughtful and Thoughtless went swimming ahead of Very Thoughtful. They did not see the fisherman's net and rushed right into it. Very Thoughtful saw them caught in the net.

"I must save them," cried Very Thoughtful. So he swam around the net. He splashed in the water in front of it. He looked like a fish that had broken through the net and gone up the river. Then he swam behind the net and splashed about. He looked like a fish that had broken through the net and gone down the river.

The fisherman saw the splashing water and thought the two fishes had broken through his net. He thought one had gone up the river and the other down. He pulled in the net by one corner. This let the two fishes escape from the net. Away they swam to find Very Thoughtful.

"You saved our lives, Very Thoughtful!" they both cried. "Now we are willing to go back to the wild country with you." That very day, they swam back to their old home and lived safely ever after.

Make Connections

When you read, you use what you already know about the subject to understand the text. You use this prior knowledge to make sense of the new information you read.

1. Read the story. Could it have happened in real life? How do you know?

   _____

   _____

2. Briefly tell about a time when you felt dumb.

   _____

   _____

3. Write one test-taking secret that you know.

   _____

4. How do you feel about taking tests?

   _____

   _____

Critical Thinking

How would reading this text be more difficult if you had never taken a test?

   _____

   _____

   _____

The Girl Who Thought She Was Dumb

Have you ever done something wrong and thought you were dumb? Everyone has that happen once in a while. However, Kara felt that way much of the time. She would get up in the morning, stumble over her slippers, and think, "I'm so dumb." She would spill her orange juice and think, "I'm so dumb."

Kara felt especially dumb at school. She would press too hard on her pencil, and the lead would break. She would do her homework and then lose it. It seemed to Kara that she never did anything right.

The thing that made Kara feel really dumb was her test scores. She usually got the lowest score in class, even though she studied. One day after school, she told the teacher how she felt. "I must be dumb," she told her. "Look at my math test. I only got four right out of 20 problems!"

"You're not dumb. You just don't know the secrets of taking tests," her teacher replied.

"There are secrets to taking tests?" asked Kara in surprise.

"Yes, there are, and if you'd like, I will teach them to you," said her teacher. "The first secret to doing well on tests is to get through the whole test. You do that by following the second secret, which is to do all the easy problems first. Skip any problems that look hard or the ones that you're not sure how to do. If you finish the test and there's still time, then go back and finish the problems you skipped."

Kara was excited. She couldn't wait until the next test. She wanted to try out her new secrets because she believed her test scores might go up. Maybe the teacher was right. Maybe she wasn't dumb after all!

Context Clues

If you come to a new word that you do not know, reread the sentence it is in. If that doesn't work, keep reading. Information that comes after the word may give you a clue as to what it means.

Scan the text for boldface words. These are the words for which you will figure out the meanings.

1. Read the text. What is the meaning of the word *fortune*?

   _____

   What clues did you use?   _____

2. What is the meaning of the word *shamrock*?

   _____

   What clues did you use?   _____

3. What is the meaning of the word *ancient*?

   _____

   What clues did you use?   _____

Critical Thinking

How did using context clues help you read this text?

_____

_____

_____

You're in Luck!

The four-leaf clover has been a symbol of good luck for hundreds of years. People around the world think it brings good **fortune**. How is it that this small green plant has come to mean so much to so many people?

The white clover is a bright green plant with three small leaves. Years ago, this plant became the national symbol of Ireland. You may know it as a **shamrock**. Once in a while, the three-leaf plant grows four leaves. No one knows why.

It's very hard to find a four-leaf clover. That's why people think if you find one, you'll have good luck. In fact, people in Wales long ago thought that the four-leaf clover was special. They used it as a charm to keep evil spirits away. Even the **ancient** Druid priests, who lived long ago in England, France, and Ireland, believed they were a sign of luck. They said that the four leaves stand for hope, love, faith, and luck.

The next time you're outside, look around for a four-leaf clover. If you're lucky, you might find one.

Context Clues

If you come to a new word that you do not know, reread the sentence it is in. If that doesn't work, keep reading. Information that comes after the word may give you a clue as to what it means.

Scan the text for boldface words. These are the words for which you will figure out the meanings.

1. Read the text. What is the meaning of the word *convenience*?

   _____

   What clues did you use? _____

2. What is the meaning of the word *contents*?

   _____

   What clues did you use? _____

3. What is the meaning of the word *fantastic*?

   _____

   What clues did you use? _____

Critical Thinking

How can using context clues help you read more difficult texts?

_____

_____

_____

Feathered Thief Boosts Business

There is a thief in Aberdeen, Scotland, and everyone knows it. But he has never been arrested. People actually cheer him on! That's because he is a seagull. Each day, he steals a bag of chips from the same **convenience** store. The seagull waits at the open door until the manager is distracted. Then he walks into the store and grabs a snack-size bag of cheese chips in his beak and rushes outdoors. Once outside, he tears the bag open. Many birds share its **contents**.

The seagull's shoplifting began one day when he first swooped into the store. Once in the store, he snatched a bag of chips. Since then, he's developed a habit. He always takes the same type of chips.

The manager is not angry. In fact, he thinks it's **fantastic**. Why? People come to watch the feathered thief make his daily grab. That's good for the store's business. And the manager does not even lose the cost of the chips because customers have begun paying for them!

Visualize

When you visualize, you form mental images based on what you read. It's like making a movie in your mind.

1. Read the first paragraph. Write three key words or phrases from the text that helped you make pictures in your mind.

   _____   _____   _____

2. Read the second paragraph. Draw the picture you made in your mind about this part of the story.

   [ ]

3. Read the last paragraph. Write three key words or phrases from the text that helped you make pictures in your mind.

   _____   _____   _____

Critical Thinking

When information is not given (for example, what Leah or Ben look like), it's okay to create a person in your mind. If the story gives you that information later, what should you do with your mental image?

_____

_____

_____

Watching Ben

One Friday after school, Leah took her three-year-old brother Ben to the park next door to their home. Ben wanted to play in the sandbox. Leah wanted to read her skateboarding magazine. Ben climbed into the sandbox. Leah sat on a nearby bench to watch him. Ben made piles with the sand. He dug tunnels through the mounds. Then he pushed his toy trucks through the tunnels. After he had done that about a dozen times, Leah decided it was safe to stop watching him. She started reading her magazine.

Suddenly, an earthworm wiggled up out of the sand. Ben saw it. Leah glanced up just then. Before she could do anything, Ben picked up the worm, popped it into his mouth, and swallowed it! Leah was so shocked that for a moment, she couldn't breathe or move. Then she jumped up, grabbed Ben, and ran home.

When Leah told their mother what happened, their mother said that swallowing a worm is disgusting but not dangerous. She said that Ben had eaten worse things. She told Leah not to worry about it, but Leah was still upset. She decided that next time, she would not take her eyes off Ben, not even for a second.

Visualize

When you visualize, you form mental images based on what you read. It's like making a movie in your mind.

1. Read the first and second paragraphs. Write three key words or phrases from the text that helped you make pictures in your mind.

   _____   _____   _____

2. Read the third paragraph. Draw the picture you made in your mind about this part of the story.

   ```




   ```

3. Read the remaining paragraphs. Write three key words of phrases from the text that helped you make pictures in your mind.

   _____   _____   _____

Critical Thinking

Visualize a place that you would like to go for a picnic. Briefly describe the place.

_____

_____

_____

A Picnic on Mars

November 15

Today, my class was able to go outside for a picnic. The weatherman said that there would be no dust storms today. No big solar flares were due until later tonight.

The air here on Mars is very thin and cold. We wore our space suits. The walk to the picnic area took only a few minutes. The red ground was very rocky, and we had to be careful not to trip over the rocks. I could see that there was a little bit of wind blowing in the pink sky. Sand blew over our feet.

Our teacher, Mrs. Ramirez, had set up a solar blanket to protect us from the sun. It was like a big umbrella. Because the air on Mars is so thin, it can't protect us from harmful rays the way the air on Earth does. We ate before we left the classroom. We couldn't eat anything at our picnic because we were all wearing our space helmets.

I found some pretty rocks for my collection. We sang some songs. We sounded funny over our space suit radios.

While we were outside, a ship from Earth landed. It held some new children coming to live on Mars with their families. I think they will like it here. It is very different from Earth, but it is very special in its own way.

Story Elements

Every story has three elements: characters, a setting, and a plot. The plot is a problem and the way it gets resolved.

1. Before you read the story, glance at each paragraph. Name the two characters.

   _____   _____

2. Read the story. Describe the setting (where and when the story happens).

   _____

   _____

3. A story's plot has two parts. The first is a conflict (problem). The second is how the problem is solved. What is the conflict in this story?

   _____

   _____

4. How is the conflict solved?

   _____

   _____

Critical Thinking

Predict what will happen next. Will Grandpa get better and go to Jamie's playoff game? Explain.

_____

_____

_____

For Grandpa

Jamie headed for the refrigerator to grab something to eat before the big game. His basketball team was doing well in the quarterfinals. He'd been practicing every chance he got and knew he was ready. This game would decide if his team would compete in the district playoffs.

Jamie ate quickly and said goodbye to his mom. He was about to walk out the door when the phone rang, surprising them both. Something in his mom's voice made Jamie turn around. He hesitated for a minute and then backtracked when he heard his mom crying.

In the kitchen, Mrs. Whitman was sitting at the table, her head buried in her arms. "What's wrong, Mama?" asked Jamie as he sat down.

"Your grandpa had a heart attack, Jamie," she said. "He is in the hospital."

Jamie couldn't believe his ears. How could his grandpa be in the hospital? They had just been together two days ago. Grandpa was fine. He was the same as he always was. Jamie would have known if his grandfather was sick.

"I'll go with you to the hospital, Mama," said Jamie.

"No, Jamie, you go and play tonight. Grandpa wouldn't want you to miss your game. I'll go to see Grandpa and meet you at home after your game," said his mother.

So Jamie went to the game and played his very best. His team won, which meant they'd go to the playoffs. As Jamie drove home with a friend, he said to himself, "That was for you, Grandpa."

Story Elements

Every story has three elements: characters, a setting, and a plot. The plot is a problem and the way it gets resolved.

1. Read the story. Describe the setting (where and when the story happens).

   _____

   _____

2. A story's plot has two parts. The first is a conflict (problem). The second is how the problem is solved. What is the conflict in this story?

   _____

   _____

3. Is the conflict solved? Explain.

   _____

   _____

   If the conflict is not solved, when will it be?

   _____

Critical Thinking

Predict what will happen next. Will Hannah do a good job at her first day at Mrs. Graff's? Explain.

_____

_____

_____

The Key

Chapter 1: The First Day

"Hannah, Hannah. It's time to wake up," William whispered in his sister's ear.

Hannah's eyes flew open. As soon as William saw her eyes open, he left. This was the girls' room. He hardly ever came in here. He and their little brothers slept in the other attic room.

Hannah's mind was still in her dream. "Find the key. Find the key," echoed in her mind.

As Hannah came to life, she remembered that this was her first day of work as a helper to Mrs. Graff at her boarding house. Worried thoughts crowded her mind. Would she do a good job? Would Mrs. Graff like her? What if she had to do something she didn't know how to do? Hannah's stomach began to churn. She was so glad that her older brother, William, would be walking with her to the boarding house.

It was just getting light outside as Hannah quietly got out of bed and stepped onto the cold wooden floor. She was careful not to wake Annie and little Lizabet. Hannah smiled as she took a moment to watch her little sisters sleep. Annie and Lizabet would have to do without her. She hoped Mother and her big sister, Mary, would pay attention to them. She knew how busy they were, though. Oh well, everyone was growing up. Annie would have to learn to take care of Lizabet. Everyone in this new country called America had to work hard.

Oh, dear. She had to stop daydreaming. Mary was already awake and downstairs. Hannah couldn't be late on the first day of work.

Plot

Every story has a plot. The plot has two parts. The first part is a problem. The second part is the way it gets resolved.

1. Read the text. What is Tim's problem in the beginning?

   _____

2. Who is Matt, and why won't he share his skateboard with Tim?

   _____

   _____

3. Why is Tim feeling discouraged before his dad talks to him?

   _____

   _____

4. What is the solution to Tim's problem?

   _____

   _____

Critical Thinking

Do you think that most stories have plots that are solved this quickly? Explain.

   _____

   _____

   _____

The Skateboard

Tim liked to watch his brother, Matt, ride his skateboard. Tim wanted to ride a skateboard, too. He asked Matt if he could borrow his board.

"No way," Tim said. "It took me months of mowing lawns to save up for this board. Get your own board!"

Tim felt sad. He didn't know how he would ever be able to have his own board.

One day, his dad said to him, "You've been looking very upset lately. What's the matter?"

"I want to ride a skateboard like Matt, but I'm too little to mow lawns," Tim sighed.

"Well," Tim's dad said, "you're also too little to ride a big board like your brother's. Instead you could probably get one just your size for less money by walking Mrs. Lukoski's dog. Mrs. Lukoski broke her ankle and won't be able to walk her dog for many weeks."

"Walk Tutu?" Tim asked. "I would love to walk Tutu!"

"Wonderful," Tim's father said. "She already called to ask me if you could, and she will pay you so that you can save for your very own skateboard."

Tim ran to see Mrs. Lukoski and then stopped. He turned around and ran back to give his dad a big hug.

As he ran to Mrs. Lukoski's house, he shouted to Matt, "I'm going to have a skateboard, too! I can't wait!"

© Shell Education

Plot

Every story has a plot. The plot has two parts. The first part is a problem. The second part is the way it gets resolved.

1. Scan the story. There are three characters mentioned. Write their names below.

   _____   _____   _____

2. Read the story. Which character is discussed but does not appear in the story?

   _____

3. What is the problem in this story?

   _____

   _____

4. Is the problem solved? Explain.

   _____

   _____

Critical Thinking

Do you think this is the end of the story? Explain.

_____

_____

_____

A Suspect Is Cleared

"How is the case going?" Principal Pallen asked Detective Dana. "Was it Lance Larkin who stole the trophy from the trophy case?"

"I don't think Lance is our thief," said Detective Dana. She flipped open her notebook. She read what she had written there.

"First, Lance is very tall. He could easily have reached the middle shelf of the trophy case without a ladder. And we know the thief used a ladder."

"Interesting," said Principal Pallen.

"Second, Lance's grandma picked him up from practice a little early that day. I don't think he would have had time to do the deed."

"I see," said Principal Pallen.

"Finally," said Detective Dana, "the glass door had candy smudges on it. The smudges turned out to be from a peanut butter cup. And Lance's teacher told me he has a peanut allergy."

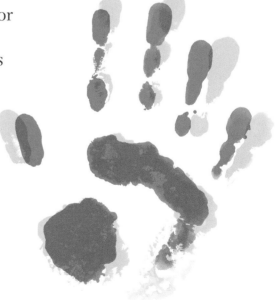

"It sounds like one of our suspects is cleared," said Principal Pallen. "Keep up the good work, Detective. I'm sure you'll have the case solved in no time."

Characters

When you read a story, it helps to think about each character. Try to picture him or her. What do you expect this character to say or do?

1. Read the story. List the characters below.

   _____

   _____

2. How is each character related to Benjamin?

   _____

   _____

3. Choose one character from the story. Tell what he or she is like.

   _____

   _____

   _____

Critical Thinking

Think of a character that you could add to this story. Name your character and tell what he or she says or does.

_____

_____

_____

Bothersome Benjamin

In the morning, Benjamin woke up and jumped out of bed. He landed beside his brother, Shane, who slept on the bottom bunk. Shane sat up and rubbed his eyes. He grumbled at Benjamin and then fell back on his bed. Then Benjamin ran to the corner and grabbed his horn. Benjamin blew his horn and played some musical notes. He liked the sound of his horn, but he heard another sound. He stopped and listened. A moan came from Shane. Benjamin disliked that sound. He grabbed his horn and ran out of the door.

He sat on the front lawn and played some more music. The notes floated in the air. He played until he heard another sound. He stopped and listened. A groan came from his next-door neighbor. Benjamin ran into the backyard. He played his horn some more. He liked the notes. Then he heard another sound. He heard his mother. She called his name again and again. He went inside. His mother took his horn and put it away. Then she told Benjamin to go back to bed. She said he had left his bed too early. Benjamin's mother went back to bed, too. Benjamin imagined the sounds of his horn.

Suddenly, he heard another sound. He listened. Shane was snoring! Benjamin moaned. He stuck his fingers in his ears, but he still heard Shane. So, he covered his head with his pillow. Soon, he fell asleep.

Characters

When you read a story, it helps to think about each character. Try to picture him or her. What do you expect this character to say or do?

1. Read the story. Name the characters.

   _____

2. What is Bear like?

   _____

   _____

3. What is Fox like?

   _____

   _____

4. What do you think Bear learned from this experience?

   _____

   _____

Critical Thinking

Which character would you rather have as a friend? Explain.

_____

_____

_____

Why Bear Has No Tail: An American Indian Legend

Long, long ago, Bear had a beautiful bushy tail. It was glossy and full, and everyone thought it was magnificent. Fox hated it. He was jealous because it was even better than his tail. He decided to play a mean trick on Bear.

Fox waited until the great pond was frozen. He cut a hole in the ice, surrounded it with fish, and then waited for Bear.

When Bear came along, he admired Fox's fish. Fox told Bear he could teach him how to catch the fish and guaranteed Bear a good catch. Bear agreed, so Fox took him to a place where he knew there were no fish and cut a hole in the ice. He instructed Bear to turn around, put his tail into the hole, and relax. He said that as long as Bear was quiet and still, the fish would come. Fox urged him to be patient. Then Fox sneaked away and went home.

In the morning, Fox went to check on Bear. Bear had fallen asleep and was covered with a dusting of new snow. Fox woke Bear up and told him it was time to pull up his tail full of fish—but the ice hole had frozen over. Bear tugged and tugged, but he couldn't pull his tail out. With one mighty yank, Bear pulled as hard as he could. And his tail came off!

Bear was furious and began to chase Fox, but Fox outran him. To this day, Bear has no tail and no love for Fox.

Title and Headings

Always read the title and headings before you read a text. They will tell you what the text will be about.

1. Look at the title and the headings. What do you think this text will be about?

   _____

   _____

2. Read the text. Write each heading and one fact from that section.

   Heading: _____

   Fact: _____

   _____

   Heading: _____

   Fact: _____

   _____

Critical Thinking

Why did the writer use headings to divide the text into sections?

_____

_____

_____

Getting the News: Then and Now

News Then

Long ago, newspapers were small, often about four pages. They had poetry, ads, and essays. There was actually very little news. Most were printed just once each week.

Few people read newspapers back then. That's because not many people could read. Most people were too busy. Often, people just told others the news they heard.

Newspapers then were hard to deliver. They were often sent only to people in the towns where they were printed. Many people shared one newspaper.

News Now

Today, people can follow the news in many ways. Many people read the news on the Internet. They may use their laptop computers or cell phones to go online. This way, people can get news very fast. There are plenty of news websites. Many people also get their news by watching TV. People like to see videos with the news. Most homes have a TV. There are many news programs. People may listen to the news on the radio while in their cars.

Of course, there are still newspapers, too. Many people read them—some on paper and some online.

Title and Headings

Always read the title and headings before you read a text. They will tell you what the text will be about.

1. Read the text. What three types of measurements are discussed?

    _____

    _____

2. Write the main idea of the section *Measuring Length*.

    _____

    _____

3. Draw a line to match each heading with its main idea.

Heading	Main Idea
Measuring Length	The Romans were the first to measure a mile.
Measuring Distance	People once used seeds to find out the volume of a container.
Measuring Volume	Hands, feet, and other body parts were used to determine how long something was.

Critical Thinking

Was the title's question answered by the text? Explain.

_____

_____

_____

WHY MEASURE?

How tall are you? How long is your house? People need to measure things. People need measurements to build things. Measurements are needed to make clothes and sell goods. In the past, people used natural things to measure. These included body parts and the sun. Stones and seeds were also used. People in different places had different ways of measuring.

Measuring Length

Long ago, people did not have measuring sticks. Instead, they used body parts—such as arms and hands—to measure length. Hands were also used to measure clothes and the height of horses. People used their body parts to measure buildings. They used their hands and arms (up to the elbow) and feet. The length of a hand and arm up to the elbow is called a *cubit*.

Measuring Distance

The Romans were the first to measure a mile. A mile was equal to 1,000 steps. Each step was 5 feet (1.5 m). So a Roman mile was 5,000 feet (1,524 m). Today, a mile is 5,280 feet (1,609.3 m).

Measuring Volume

It is important to know the volume of a container. Imagine that you wanted to buy a container of rice. You would want to know how big the container was before you paid. That way, you would know if you were getting a good deal. In the past, people used seeds to measure the volume of a container. The seeds were poured into the container until it was full. Then the seeds were counted.

Typeface and Captions

A caption is a title or a sentence given for an illustration. Words are set in a typeface. It can be normal, boldface, or italic. Sometimes words are underlined. When you see text set in one of these ways, it is a special typeface. It means the word is important.

1. Scan the text. What special typeface do you see in the first line of text?

    _____

2. Which words are set in that special typeface?

    _____

3. Write a new caption that tells what the people in the picture are doing.

    _____

    _____

    _____

Critical Thinking

Look at the title at the top of the page. What might the title mean?

_____

_____

_____

Not So Different

Long ago in **colonial times**, people lived and worked in small towns and in the country. Children studied, did chores, and played when they could. Most families grew their own food. They ate meals together and went to church together. They took care of each other.

Colonial times were the times before the United States became a country, when people were trying to build a life far away from their home countries in Europe.

Typeface and Captions

A caption is a title or a sentence given for an illustration. Words are set in a typeface. It can be normal, boldface, or italic. Sometimes words can be underlined. When you see text set in one of these ways, it is a special typeface. It means the word is important.

1. Look at the title at the top of the page. What might the title mean?

   _____

2. Scan the text. What is the special typeface you see on words in the second and third paragraphs?

   _____

3. Write the words that are set in that special typeface.

   _____   _____

4. Read the text. How do the captions help you understand what you read?

   _____

   _____

Critical Thinking

Imagine that you took a photograph of your mom or dad riding a big tricycle. Write a caption for the photograph.

_____

_____

_____

Bike Beginnings

Kids and bikes just seem to go together. It's hard to imagine childhood without bikes. But bikes as we know them have only been around for about 150 years. And the earliest bikes weren't really for kids. Only the most daring adults rode them.

Boneshakers

One of the first bikes was the *velocipede*. It was popular in 1865. These bikes were made all of wood. They were really heavy. Most people called them "boneshakers." That's because they bump-bump-bumped on cobblestone roads. Adults went to "riding academies" to learn how to ride their bikes. These academies were like roller skating rinks. The people paid to take lessons there.

Big Wheel, Big Deal

The next type of bike to become popular was the *penny-farthing*. These metal bikes were first made in 1870. A penny-farthing had a huge front wheel and a tiny back wheel. The front wheel was often about five feet high. Adults climbed on stools to get on these bikes. (And if they fell off, it was a long way down!) Only rich people could buy these bikes. They cost what most workers made in six months.

penny-farthing

Adults on Tricycles

Adult tricycles were a big hit back then, too. People thought that trikes were more ladylike than bikes. Rich women rode them. Doctors and preachers liked them, too. They rode their trikes to people's homes. Can you picture your mom or dad riding on a big tricycle?

adult tricycle

Graphics

Always look at the pictures, maps, or diagrams before you read the text. They will give you clues as to what the text will be about.

1. Preview the text. Look at the picture under the title. What is shown in the picture?

   _____

2. What is shown in the graphic at the bottom of the page?

   _____

3. Read the text. Then answer these questions using the graphic with the title *Earth's Closest Stars*.

   How many stars are shown? _____

   Which star is farthest from Earth? _____

   How many miles away is Barnard's Star? _____

Critical Thinking

Is the object in the picture under the title natural or manmade? How do you know?

_____

_____

_____

OUTER SPACE

We see many stars in the sky. They are all very far away. Our sun is the star nearest to Earth. It is 93 million miles (149.7 million km) away. The picture below shows the five stars that are closest to Earth.

Think about looking into the sky at night. It looks as if all the stars are close together in space. But they are not. Space is really big. It's so big it is hard for us to imagine. Our galaxy, the Milky Way, is just one part of it. It takes a ray of light 100,000 years to travel across the Milky Way. This means that each star has plenty of room around it.

Earth's Closest Stars

Proxima Centaur 25 trillion miles (40.2 trillion km)

Wolf 359 46 trillion miles (74 trillion km)

Alpha Centauri 26 trillion miles (41.8 trillion km)

Barnard's Star 35 trillion miles (56.3 trillion km)

Sun

Earth

Graphics

Always look at the pictures, maps, or diagrams before you read the text. They will give you clues as to what the text will be about.

1. Preview the text. What is shown in the illustration of the person?

    _____

    _____

2. The inset is the enlarged part of the picture inside the circle. What is shown in the inset?

    _____

3. Read the text. Then use the graphic to help you answer these questions:

    Is your diaphragm above or below your heart? _____

    Is your liver behind or in front of your lungs? _____

    Is your trachea inside or outside your lungs? _____

Critical Thinking

How does the diagram help you to understand how your lungs work?

_____

_____

_____

Your Lungs and How They Work

You have two lungs in your chest on each side of your heart. They look like soft, wet, pink-gray sponges. Breathe in deeply, and you will see your chest rise. This is because your lungs are filling with air. Breathe out and your chest lowers. This is your lungs releasing the air.

You need to breathe in order to stay alive. You breathe to get oxygen. Breathing pulls air into your nose and down your *trachea*. Your trachea carries the air through tubes that look like the branches of an upside-down tree. The tubes are called *bronchi*. They take the oxygen from the air and move it into to your blood. Then your blood moves all through your body, bringing the oxygen to all your cells.

Your body knows how much air it needs. If you run hard or get scared, you will breathe faster to get more oxygen. At night, when you are asleep, you do not need very much oxygen. You breathe slowly when you are asleep.

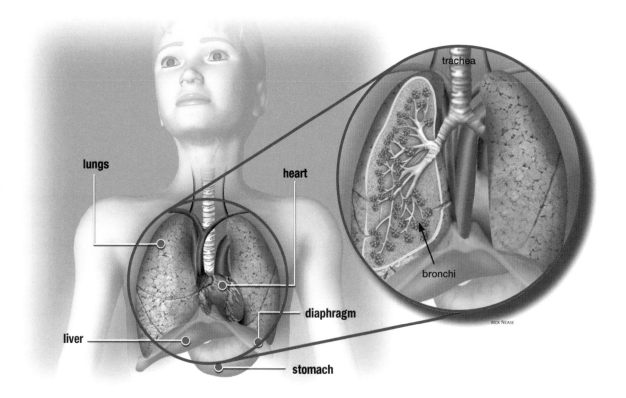

Topic Sentences

A topic sentence is one that sums up what the paragraph is about. It is often, but not always, the first sentence in a paragraph.

1. Read the text. Write the topic sentence of the first paragraph.

    _____

    _____

2. Write the topic sentence of the second paragraph.

    _____

    _____

3. Create a topic sentence for the third paragraph.

    _____

    _____

Critical Thinking

How will you use what you know about topic sentences the next time you read a nonfiction text?

_____

_____

_____

THE CARIBBEAN SEA

The Caribbean Sea is a pretty place. The warm water has many shades of blue and green. There are many kinds of fish and turtles. It has many islands. The islands are alive with beauty. The sea also has many coral reefs.

The Caribbean Sea is actually a part of the Atlantic Ocean. It is very large. It is about 1,500 miles (2,414 km) across. It is 900 (1,448 km) miles wide. That is a big sea!

Long ago, other countries wanted to control the Caribbean. They fought over the islands. Now some of the islands belong to other nations. Some of the islands are their own nations.

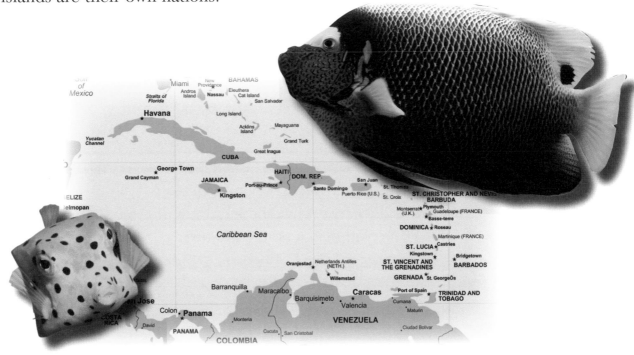

Topic Sentences

A topic sentence is one that sums up what the paragraph is about. It is often, but not always, the first sentence in a paragraph.

1. Read the text. Write the topic sentence of the second paragraph.

   _____

2. Write the topic sentence of the third paragraph.

   _____

3. Write the topic sentence of the last paragraph.

   _____

   Why is this topic sentence in a different position in the paragraph than the other topic sentences?

   _____

   _____

Critical Thinking

How will you use what you know about topic sentences the next time you read a nonfiction text?

_____

_____

_____

Be a Responsible Consumer!

Use it up.
Wear it out.
Make it do
Or do without.

This is an old saying that still holds true today. We need to be responsible for our environment. Being a frugal consumer is one way to help. But, what exactly does that mean?

Use It Up

You can use things up instead of wasting them. Squeeze that last bit of toothpaste out of the tube. Use the last little sliver of soap. Don't throw away the flakes at the bottom of the cereal box.

Wear It Out

You do not always need to have new things. Suppose your sneakers have broken laces, but they still fit you. Replace the laces and wear them longer. You don't have to have the latest electronic gadget. Use your MP3 player until it quits. Then you can get a new one. Think twice before replacing something that still works.

Make It Do

When something you want is not available, look for something else that you already have to take its place. Suppose you are packing your lunch for tomorrow and want a peanut butter sandwich. You are out of peanut butter. Have a cheese sandwich instead so that you can use all of the cheese. Learn to fix broken toys instead of just tossing them out. With a little thought, you can make something do, instead of buying something new.

Do Without

Think about all those things that you would like to have. Do you really need them? How long will you really play with that new toy you saw on TV? Making the things that we want uses up our world's resources. And, getting rid of the things we don't want any more takes up even more resources and space. By being responsible consumers, we help our environment.

Main Idea

The main idea is what a text is mostly about. Sometimes the main idea is stated in a sentence in the text. That sentence is usually the first—and sometimes the last—sentence in a paragraph.

1. Scan the first sentence of each paragraph. Often this sentence states the main idea of that paragraph. Write the main idea of the passage in the graphic organizer below.

2. Read the text. Fill in the graphic organizer with details that support the main idea. Write one detail in each box below.

Main Idea		
Detail	**Detail**	**Detail**

Critical Thinking

How did scanning the text first help you to find the main idea sentence quickly as you read the text?

_____

_____

_____

Seahorses

A seahorse is a strange kind of fish. Its head looks a lot like a horse's head, but it is not as big as a horse. A seahorse can be as small as about half an inch (1.3 cm) or as big as two feet (0.6 m) long. It likes to live in warm waters and hardly ever swims, which is pretty unusual for a fish.

A seahorse has a tail like a monkey's and uses it to hold onto sea plants. It waits for food to come floating by. A seahorse eats the tiny shrimp and baby fish that come close enough.

This may be the strangest seahorse fact of all: a seahorse dad, not the mom, gives birth to baby seahorses! He has about one hundred babies at one time. That's a lot of babies! It's hard to believe that a seahorse is called a fish.

Main Idea

The main idea is what a text is mostly about. Sometimes the main idea is stated in a sentence in the text. That sentence is usually the first—and sometimes the last—sentence in a paragraph.

Scan the first and last sentence of each paragraph. One of these sentences is the main idea.

1. Read the text. Write the main idea below.

   _____

   _____

2. The main idea is supported by details in the second and third paragraphs. Write four of those details below.

   _____

   _____

   _____

   _____

Critical Thinking

How did scanning the text first help you to find the main idea sentence quickly as you read the text?

_____

_____

_____

The Octopus

Imagine that you're going diving. You get your gear on and get into the water. The ocean water is cold, but you don't care. There have been reports of a giant octopus in the area. You want to see it for yourself. You swim down amidst the schools of fish. A movement catches your eye. There it is! A giant octopus! You are excited and a little bit scared.

The octopus is an awesome sea creature. There are about 50 kinds of octopuses. They range from 3 inches (7 cm) to 10 feet (3 m) in length. The larger ones can weigh 70 pounds (32 kg). The big ones are quite strong. They can grab a full-grown human and drag him or her down to the bottom of the sea. Gulp!

Octopuses, no matter which kind, look and behave similarly. They all have eight arms. Each arm has rows of suckers. And if they lose one of their arms, another one will grow back! Octopuses swim or walk on the very ends of their arms, as if they're dancing. Their bodies move fluidly because they have no bones. They can hide on the rocks by changing their color. When they are afraid of attack, they spray purple ink. While the predator is confused by the cloud in the water, the octopus escapes.

You don't need a wetsuit and diving gear to see one of these fascinating creatures. Just visit your nearest aquarium.

Details

As you read, ask yourself, "What is this story about?" That is the main idea. Then you can find the details that support the main idea.

1. Read the text. Write the main idea in the center of the web below.

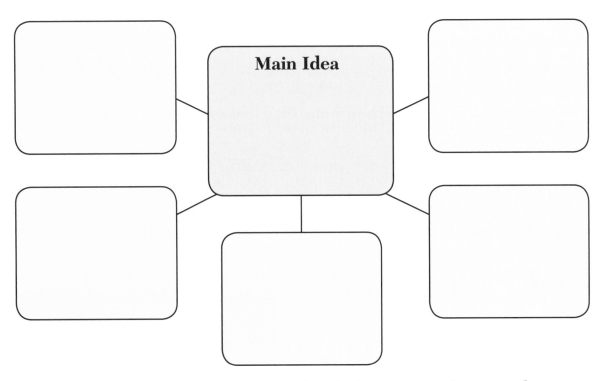

Main Idea

2. Reread the text. Then write five details that support the main idea in the boxes that surround the main idea.

Critical Thinking

How do the details in a fiction (not true) story differ from the details in a nonfiction (true) text?

_____

_____

_____

© Shell Education

Cyber Kids to the Rescue

As Nell whirled around, she shrunk. She became quite tiny. She quickly hopped onto her magic mouse pad. Right click! She was on her way to pick up Chan.

Landing near Chan's computer was always a challenge. Rarely was there an area clear enough for a level landing. Oh well, she needed his brains. This case was going to be a tough one.

Chan caught her just before she fell off his desk and said, "Hi, Nell. What's up?"

"We need to fix Olga's computer. It's got a very bad virus."

"Never fear; Chan is here!"

"Oh, just get small and jump on. Olga lives in the Ukraine!"

Through the darkness of cyberspace the pair flew, landing deep inside the hard drive of a computer far across the globe. Nell and Chan donned their antivirus fighting gear and got to work.

Hours later, Nell was back to normal size and getting ready for school. She knew that her classmates would never believe where she had been—even if she wanted to tell them.

© Shell Education

Details

As you read, ask yourself, "What is this text about?" That is the main idea. Then you can find the details that support the main idea.

1. The main idea is not directly stated in this text. You will have to figure it out. Read the text.

2. In the table below, write the main idea at the top. Then write four details that support the main idea. Write one detail in each section.

Main Idea
Detail
Detail
Detail
Detail

Critical Thinking

How do the details in a fiction (not true) story differ from the details in a nonfiction (true) text?

_____

_____

_____

Help Is Just a Click Away

"Hey, Mom, I don't get how to do this math problem."

"How does your book say to do it?"

"I don't understand the book."

"Okay, let me see. Hmm, I don't understand it either. That's not how we learned to do it. Ask your father."

Do conversations like this happen at your house? There is a way to find help. Use the Internet! There are many homework helper websites. One of them will probably show you how to do your math problem in a way that you can understand.

Have an adult with you the first time you go looking for help. This will make sure you find safe, kid-friendly sites. There are sites for all subjects. Some sites have animated videos teaching about a topic. Others have ways to ask questions, and a real person will email you an answer. Some sites provide ideas and resources for projects.

There is a whole lot of information out there! Find several sites that work for you. Then bookmark them so they are easy to return to later. That way, the next time you get stuck on a homework problem, you will know what to do. Just click on your favorite site and get some free help!

© Shell Education

Main Idea and Details

When you read, decide what the text is mostly about. That is the main idea. The main idea is supported by details. Some of the details are important. Others are not as important.

1. Read the text. Write one example of a fad.

   _____

2. Write the main idea of the text in the graphic organizer below. In the smaller sections, write the details that support the main idea. Include the three *most important* details.

Main Idea		
Detail	**Detail**	**Detail**

Critical Thinking

How did you decide which details to include and which to leave out?

_____

_____

_____

Fad-tastic Fads

Silly toys. Goofy hairstyles. Funny dances. Every year seems to have its fads.

A fad is something that happens fast. All of a sudden, everyone wants to have it or do it. Then the fad usually ends as quickly as it started. Do you remember those little stuffed animal pets? You could go online to feed and walk them. Every kid seemed to have one. They were a fad.

Ask your mom or dad about fads they remember. Ask your grandma and grandpa, too. You might hear about toys such as Rubik's Cubes, Cabbage Patch Dolls®, and pet rocks. Hula-hoops were a big toy fad in the 1950s. In the 1980s, kids and teens loved Pac-Man. This video game was so popular that a song about it also became a hit.

Hairstyles and clothes can be fads, too. So can jewelry. Your mom and grandma might remember mood rings or toe socks. They might tell you how they once wore their hair "feathered" to look like actress Farrah Fawcett. Back then, everyone wanted "big hair."

Sometimes, the fad is something you do. Gulping down live goldfish was a fad in 1939. Teens held contests. The winner was whoever swallowed the most fish. Eww! Break dancing was a fad in the 1980s. Everyone tried to do a dance step called the moonwalk. Singer Michael Jackson had made it famous.

What are the fads at your school right now? What do you think the next fad will be?

Time Order

Putting events in the time order in which they occurred is called chronological order. It tells the events from start to finish. It is a good way to organize what happened in a text.

1. Read the text. Then number the sentences in the correct order from 1–4 (first to last).

   _____ Corey throws seaweed on the writer.

   _____ Corey feels sea spray.

   _____ Grandpa throws seaweed on Corey.

   _____ Grandpa tells Corey about sea shells.

2. Write an event that could come next.

   _____

   _____

3. Why was it good that this story was written in chronological order?

   _____

   _____

Critical Thinking

Do you think this was the end of the diary entry? Explain.

_____

_____

_____

Seaweed Scare

Wednesday, July 25

Today, my grandpa and my friend, Corey, and I took a walk on the beach. Corey was excited because he had never been to the beach before. He wanted to see a shell. I told him that he could see them all around on the sand. They were those hard little shapes he was stepping on. Grandpa told him about how animals had once lived inside the shells. He told us about how the hard shells protected the animals inside. A wave broke, and we felt the sea spray.

"Did you feel that?" I asked Corey.

"It felt like someone sprayed my face with a spray bottle," Corey laughed.

My grandpa winked at me. He held his finger up to his mouth so that I wouldn't say anything. I knew my grandpa was going to play a trick on Corey. Suddenly he threw some seaweed at us and yelled that it was a sea monster about to grab us by our throats!

Corey screamed and grabbed his own throat to protect it from the sea monster. I was so startled that I grabbed my own throat, too, and almost choked myself in the struggle! When Corey saw me grabbing my throat, he started to laugh.

"It's just some silly seaweed," my grandpa told us.

"Yeah, but YOU thought it was over for you!" Corey said to me, and he tossed some more seaweed at me.

Time Order

Putting events in the time order in which they occurred is called chronological order. It tells the events from start to finish. It is a good way to organize what happened in a text.

1. Read the text. Number the sentences in the correct order from 1–5 (first to last).

    _____ Scotty's Castle was built.

    _____ Death Valley was made a national monument.

    _____ People came to Death Valley to mine gold.

    _____ American Indians came to Death Valley.

    _____ People began mining borax in Death Valley.

2. On the time line, write what happened in Death Valley for each date.

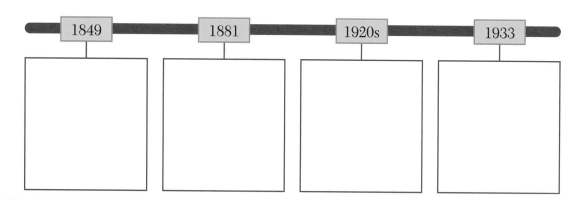

1849	1881	1920s	1933

Critical Thinking

Why do authors write events in chronological order?

_____

_____

_____

DEATH VALLEY

Death Valley is a desert in the United States. It is hot and dry. American Indians came to Death Valley long ago. But they did not live there all year. Sometimes they camped and hunted in other places. Sometimes they did not go to Death Valley for many years. Today, you can find the things they left behind. You might find arrowheads and spearheads. You might find bits of pottery, too.

In 1849, other people came to Death Valley. They were looking for gold. They did not plan well for their trip. It was very hot and dry. Many people died in Death Valley. That is how it got its name.

More people came to Death Valley in 1881. They came to mine borax. Borax is a chemical. It is used for cleaning and to make certain products. People picked up or dug borax pieces from the ground. The borax was packed and taken to the city of Mojave. Mules moved the borax.

Scotty's Castle is a famous place in Death Valley. It is a ranch house. Albert Johnson built the house in the 1920s. It was named for Walter Scott, a miner who was Johnson's friend. People called him "Death Valley Scotty."

Death Valley is famous for its beauty. People want it to stay beautiful and natural. That is why it was made a national monument in 1933.

Logical Order

Logical order is putting information in an order that makes sense. For example, you would tell how to make a cake in the order in which you would add the ingredients.

1. Read the story. Think about what Patty wanted to do with the money she got from selling the milk.

2. Write Patty's plans in logical order.

```
┌─────────────────────────────────────────────────┐
│                                                   │
└─────────────────────────────────────────────────┘
                        ↓
┌─────────────────────────────────────────────────┐
│                                                   │
└─────────────────────────────────────────────────┘
                        ↓
┌─────────────────────────────────────────────────┐
│                                                   │
└─────────────────────────────────────────────────┘
                        ↓
┌─────────────────────────────────────────────────┐
│                                                   │
└─────────────────────────────────────────────────┘
                        ↓
┌─────────────────────────────────────────────────┐
│                                                   │
└─────────────────────────────────────────────────┘
                        ↓
┌─────────────────────────────────────────────────┐
│                                                   │
└─────────────────────────────────────────────────┘
```

Critical Thinking

Think about what Patty's mother said. What did she mean?

_____

_____

_____

Patty the Milkmaid

One morning Patty, a milkmaid, was going to market. On her head, she carried milk in a pail. As she walked along, she made a plan. She thought about what she would do with the money she would get from selling the milk.

"I'll buy some chickens from Farmer McCall," she thought to herself. "The chickens will lay eggs each morning. I will sell those eggs to the baker's wife. With the money that I get from selling the eggs, I will buy myself a beautiful dress and a fancy hat with a feather. Then when I go to market, all the young men will notice me and talk to me. That will make Polly Shaw jealous, but I don't care. I'll just look at her and show off my hat by tossing my head like this."

When Patty tossed her head, the pail fell off. The milk poured all over the ground. Patty was upset. She went home and told her mother what had happened.

"Oh my child," her mother said, "Don't count your chickens before they are hatched."

© Shell Education

Logical Order

Logical order is putting information in an order that makes sense. For example, you would tell how to make a cake in the order in which you would add the ingredients.

1. Think about an ice cream sundae you have had. List the ingredients.

   _____

2. Read the text. How did the writer make the ice cream sundae? Write the steps in order:

   Step 1: _____

   Step 2: _____

   Step 3: _____

   Step 4: _____

   Step 5: _____

   Step 6: _____

   Step 7: _____

Critical Thinking

If you were making your own whipped cream, where would that step go in the sequence above?

_____

_____

_____

How to Make an Ice Cream Sundae

An ice cream sundae is a good treat, no matter what the weather. Here are simple instructions you can follow on your own to make a delicious ice cream sundae.

You'll need ice cream, chocolate sauce (or caramel or any other sauce you like), chopped nuts, cherries, and whipped cream. You can buy whipped cream in a can or in a plastic tub, or you can make your own. If you make your own, though, make it ahead of time.

To begin, get out a bowl, a spoon, and all of the above ingredients.

Choose your favorite flavor of ice cream. Use the spoon to scoop out a good-size serving and put it in the bowl. Pour some of the sauce on top of the ice cream. If you're using hot fudge, ask an adult to help you heat it up. Then sprinkle the nuts over the sundae. You can use any kind of nuts you like, but peanuts or pecans are especially good.

Shake up the can of whipped cream, turn the can upside down, and press the lever on the spout until the whipped cream comes out. Top your sundae with a maraschino cherry or a strawberry. Then dig in! Yum!

Oh, and one more thing—clean up after yourself. Put everything away and wipe up any spills you made. It will show your parents that you're responsible, so they're more likely to say "yes" the next time you ask to make a sundae.

Fact and Opinion

A fact is something that can be proven. An opinion is what someone thinks. Today is rainy is a fact. You can prove it by looking outside. Rainy days are wonderful is an opinion. Not everyone would agree!

1. Read the letter. Write one fact from it.

   _____

2. Write one opinion from the letter.

   _____

3. Read each statement. Mark it *F* for Fact or *O* for Opinion.

   _____ A parade marched through the streets.

   _____ The Hanshin Tigers are a professional baseball team in Japan.

   _____ Tomo's baseball card collection is better than mine.

   _____ Ronin has a brother.

   _____ You should go to the circus if you get the chance.

Critical Thinking

What is Ronin's opinion about grandparents living with grandkids?

_____

_____

_____

Letter to My Pen Pal

May 8

Dear Pen Pal,

I love to go to the circus! On May 6, one came to my town. A parade marched through the streets. My best friend, Kenji, and I went to watch the circus performers get ready for opening night. We saw clowns, acrobats, and even the ringmaster. It was the best fun! Have you ever seen a circus? You should go if you get the chance.

I also really like playing baseball. My favorite team is the Hanshin Tigers. They are the best team in the league. The Yomiuri Giants are terrific, too. When I grow up, I want to be a baseball pitcher, first baseman, or shortstop. Do you play baseball? What do you want to do when you grow up? I wish you could see my cool baseball card collection. My friend Tomo's collection is even better than mine.

Oh, I almost forgot to tell you about my family. There are four people: my mom, my dad, my brother, and me. In August, my grandpa will move in with us. I can't wait! Doesn't your grandma live with you? I bet it's a lot of fun.

Well, that's all for now. Please write back.

Your pal,

Ronin

Svetlana Larina / Shutterstock, Inc.

Fact and Opinion

A fact is something that can be proven. An opinion is what someone thinks. Today is rainy is a fact. You can prove it by looking outside. Rainy days are wonderful is an opinion. Not everyone would agree!

1. Read the text. Write one fact from it.

   _____

2. Write one opinion from the text.

   _____

3. Read each statement. Mark it *F* for Fact or *O* for Opinion.

   _____ The wood from the maple makes the most beautiful furniture.

   _____ Maple syrup and maple sugar are made from the sap of a maple tree.

   _____ The tree's bark is flaky and gray.

   _____ If you are looking for the best kind of tree to plant in your yard, choose the sugar maple.

   _____ In the autumn, the maple tree drops its leaves.

Critical Thinking

What opinion does the writer want you to have about the sugar maple tree? How do you know?

_____

_____

_____

The Sugar Maple Tree

The sugar maple is a wonderful tree. Both maple syrup and maple sugar are made from its sap. Its wood has a nice grain pattern. It makes the most beautiful furniture. It also makes a perfect shade tree. People plant sugar maples in their yards and along their streets. No wonder it is one of our favorite trees.

The bark of the tree is flaky and gray. Birds and squirrels eat its seeds. Each fall, the leaves of the sugar maple turn a rich yellow, orange, or red. They look as if someone had painted them with a giant brush. Later in autumn, the tree drops its leaves. It stands bare.

The sugar maple grows mainly in the middle and eastern states. It reaches 75–100 feet (22.8–30.5 m) in height. There are many kinds of maple trees. The black maple, red maple, and silver maple are just a few of the 60 varieties. But if you are looking for the best kind of tree to plant in your yard, choose the sugar maple.

Proposition and Support

A proposition is a writer's opinion. The writer wants the reader to agree. So the writer gives support (reasons and information) to get the reader to share the same opinion.

1. Read the title. What do you think the proposition will be?

   _____

   _____

2. Read the text. What is the writer's proposition?

   _____

   _____

3. Write at least three supporting details (reasons or facts) for the writer's proposition.

   _____

   _____

   _____

Critical Thinking

Did the writer persuade you to agree that people should wear pajamas to school? Explain.

   _____

   _____

   _____

Pajamas Belong at School

We should wear pajamas to school. There are several good reasons why. If we wear pajamas to school, we will be warm and comfortable. We will feel safe. If we feel warm and safe, we will do better work in the classroom. Plus, fewer of us would miss the bus if we didn't have to get dressed in the morning. If it is cold outside, we could wear robes and slippers, too.

It would be good to be in our pajamas while our teacher reads to us. Maybe we could have hot chocolate during story time. School would be more fun, too, because pajamas are colorful. Maybe our teachers would like to come to school in pajamas, too!

Proposition and Support

A proposition is a writer's opinion. The writer wants the reader to agree. So the writer gives support (reasons and information) to get the reader to share the same opinion.

1. Read the title. What do you think the proposition will be?

    _____

    _____

2. Read the text. What is the writer's proposition?

    _____

    _____

3. Write at least three supporting details (reasons or facts) for the writer's proposition.

    _____

    _____

    _____

Critical Thinking

How is proposition and support similar to a writer stating a problem and offering a solution?

_____

_____

_____

EATING RIGHT

You have choices about what you eat. The choices you make are important. Eating right means eating healthy food. What do you usually eat for snacks and meals? It is okay to eat some treats, but not too often.

Fruits and vegetables are better for you than cookies and candy. Try to eat a "rainbow" of fruits and vegetables each day. Eat red cherries, orange mangos, and yellow bananas. Then add green broccoli, blueberries, and purple grapes. These foods contain lots of vitamins and minerals. These nutrients help to keep you healthy.

Bread, nuts, and milk are good, too. They are good sources of protein. Protein helps your body to build muscles and bone. It will help your body stay strong.

Your body needs healthy food. Put good food on your plate to make a healthy meal. Your body will thank you.

Author's Purpose

When you read, ask yourself why the author wrote the text.
Read carefully to determine the author's view about the topic.

1. Read the text. Why did the author write this text?

   _____

   _____

2. How does the author feel about air shows? How do you know?

   _____

   _____

   _____

3. What part of an air show might the author disapprove of?

   _____

   _____

Critical Thinking

How might the author respond to a person who says there should be no air shows because of the noise they create?

_____

_____

_____

Exciting Air Shows

Airplanes overhead climbing and diving, jet planes flying close together wing to wing, crowds cheering and clapping—that is the fun of going to an air show.

From the time of the early planes, there have been air shows. Most of the early planes had two sets of wings. They are called *biplanes*. (*Bi-* means "two.") The pilots sat in open seats called *cockpits*. They wore goggles to protect their eyes and heavy jackets to stay warm.

The pilots did many tricks with their planes. They would fly straight up. Then they would dive nose down and go roaring over the crowd. Sometimes a man or a woman would stand on one of the wings as the airplane flew. They had only straps on their feet to hold them on! Then when the plane rolled over, they would hang upside down. This was a very dangerous trick.

Many of the old planes fly in air shows even today. If you are lucky enough to go to an air show, you may see one of these old planes.

Author's Purpose

When you read, ask yourself why the author wrote the text. Read carefully to determine the author's view about the topic.

1. Read the text. Why did the author write this text?

   _____

   _____

2. How does the author feel about kids having time to relax?

   _____

   _____

3. If the school week were four days long, what would the author want kids to do on Fridays?

   _____

   _____

   _____

Critical Thinking

How might the author respond to a person who says there should be school six days a week, like in China?

_____

_____

_____

Wanted: *Relaxation*

You may have school, soccer practice, and piano. You may have dance class, gymnastics, chess club, and art class. Everyone's so busy each day. There's no time for kids to relax anymore.

Why not change the rules? What if kids went to school for four days a week instead of five? On Fridays, everyone would have the day off just to do fun things. They could play with their friends and relax. They could watch movies or play video games. Or, they could just do nothing. Kids need vacation time, too—and not just in the summer. No extra classes or sports would be offered to kids on Fridays.

If kids had Fridays off, they could sleep late instead of getting up when it's still dark. The school district would save money. They wouldn't have to pay for buses, salaries, or electricity on those days.

If kids had an extra day off, they would work harder at school the rest of the week. Teachers could use that day to learn new ways of doing things in class. They could help each other solve problems. They could plan new activities. Everyone would benefit, and the kids who don't like school much might start to like it better.

Compare and Contrast

When you compare, you ask yourself how things are the same.
When you contrast, you focus on how things are different.

1. Read the text. On the chart, write a fact about each animal.

Kangaroo	Rabbit
Ears:	Ears:
Legs:	Legs:
Where they live:	Where they live:
Babies:	Babies:
Size:	Size:
Color:	Color:
Tail:	Tail:

2. How would a kangaroo and a rabbit look side by side? Draw a picture to show your answer.

Critical Thinking

Are kangaroos and rabbits more alike or more different? Explain.

_____

_____

_____

What Goes Hop, Hop, Hop?........

When you hear hop, hop, hop, what comes to mind? Is it a rabbit, a kangaroo, or both?

Both rabbits and kangaroos have tall ears that point straight up. Both animals hop on their large hind legs. However, a rabbit's front feet touch the ground, and a kangaroo's do not! A kangaroo's front legs are too short and look like arms.

Rabbits can be found all over the world, while kangaroos only live in Australia. Which one do you think you have a better chance of seeing?

A baby rabbit is called a kit. A baby kangaroo is called a joey. Most kits live in underground nests with their mother. A joey will live in its mother's pouch. That's a pocket in the front of her body.

Kangaroos have big legs and long, strong tails. Some can be as tall as 6 feet (1.8 m). They may weigh over 100 pounds (45.3 km). They can have brown, red, or gray fur. Rabbits are much, much smaller. Most weigh less than 5 pounds (2.3 km). They have very short, fluffy tails. When they're not hopping, rabbits sit on their front and hind legs. Most rabbits will grow less than 2 feet (0.6 m) long. They usually have brown and gray fur.

Now that you know more about them, which animal would you ask to just hop on over?

Compare and Contrast

When you compare, you ask yourself how things are the same.
When you contrast, you focus on how things are different.

1. Read the text. On the chart, write a fact about each animal.

Sarcosuchus of Long Ago	Crocodile of Today
Head:	Head:
Skin:	Skin:
Tail:	Tail:
Size:	Size:
Prey:	Prey:

2. How would a *Sarcosuchus* and a modern crocodile look side by side?
   Draw and label a picture to show your answer.

Critical Thinking

Are *Sarcosuchus* and a modern crocodile more alike or more different? Explain.

_____

_____

_____

One Big Croc

Fossils of a giant crocodile have been discovered in Africa. Scientists have named the croc Sarcosuchus (sar-ko-SOOK-us). Sarcosuchus lived long ago. It looked very much like crocodiles of today.

It had a long head filled with sharp teeth. Its skin was covered with tough, thick scales. It had a strong tail for swimming. Crocodiles today share those things. However, Sarcosuchus was much bigger than crocs are today. It was about 50 feet (15.2 m) long. That's about the length of your school bus! The biggest crocs today are more like 16 feet (4.9 m). That's about the length of a living room.

Today's crocodiles eat prey. They attack animals like deer and water buffalo when they come to a river to drink. Sarcosuchus ate bigger prey. It attacked large dinosaurs when they came to drink. It was one big, scary croc!

Classify

*Sometimes when you read, you find groups that go together.
For example, you can group shapes, colors, or animals.*

1. Read the text. Then write each of the following activities under the heading for the kind of bike that would most likely be used.

   - riding at a beach
   - competing in a dirt bike race
   - racing on roads for a long distance
   - riding with a friend
   - doing tricks on ramps

10-Speed Bikes	BMX Bikes	Tandem Bikes

Critical Thinking

What is an activity that you could use any kind of bike to do?

_____

_____

_____

Bikes, Bikes, Bikes

Do you ride a bike? What kind of bike do you have? Having a bike means different things to different people. To some, riding a bike is just a fun thing to do. To others, it means freedom. It's a way you can get yourself from one place to another without someone else having to take you there. Some people even use their bikes to earn money.

10-Speed Bikes

More 10-speed bikes are made in the United States than any other kind of bike. You change gears to make it easier to ride up and down hills.

BMX Bikes

BMX bikes are also known as dirt bikes. They became popular in the 1960s with kids who weren't old enough to ride motorcycles. BMX bikes can now be seen on all kinds of roads. There are no gears to shift on a BMX bike.

Tandem Bikes

Tandem bikes are built for two people. These bikes have two seats and two sets of handlebars. People ride tandem bikes around parks, at beaches, or in bicycling races.

Which kind of bike would you most like to ride?

10-speed bike   **BMX bike**   **tandem bike**

Classify

Sometimes when you read, you find groups that go together. For example, you can group shapes, colors, or animals.

1. Look at the title and the first sentence. What kind of groups do you think you will read about in this text?

   _____

2. Read the text. Then fill in the graphic organizer. Write the title in the box at the top. Label each box with a category. Then add details.

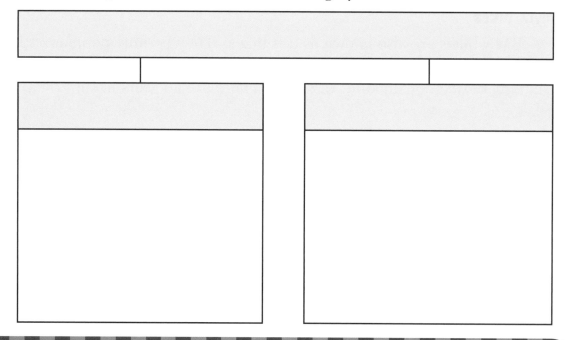

Critical Thinking

How did listing the information in categories help you to understand what you read?

_____

_____

_____

Dino Predators Big and Small

Fierce dinosaurs came in all shapes and sizes. Some of them were very small. *Velociraptor* (vuh-LOSS-uh-RAP-tor) was a dinosaur the size of a big dog. It hunted other dinosaurs in packs. It used its sharp teeth to tear its prey apart. *Ceratosaurus* (suh-RAT-oh-sore-us) was larger than *Velociraptor*. It had a crest on its nose. Its teeth were even bigger and sharper.

Some meat-eating dinosaurs were very big. *Tyrannosaurus* (tie-RAN-oh-sore-us) was a giant dinosaur that ate other dinosaurs. For a long time, scientists believed it must be at the very top of the food chain. Then *Giganotosaurus* (jig-uh-NOTE-oh-sore-us) was discovered. It was even bigger than *Tyrannosaurus*. It is one of the longest meat-eating dinosaurs found so far. It must have hunted the largest plant eaters.

Cause and Effect

A cause makes something happen. The effect is what happens. When you read, notice cause-and-effect relationships. This will help you to understand how and why things occur.

This text will tell you how a zipper works. Look for the cause and effect.

1. Read the text. What causes a zipper's "teeth" to move together?

   _____

   _____

2. What is the effect (result) of pulling a zipper slide down?

   _____

   _____

3. What do you think people used for closures before zippers were invented? (Hint: Some are mentioned in the text.)

   _____

   _____

Critical Thinking

Why did people switch to using zippers from other kinds of fasteners?

_____

_____

_____

Zippety Doo Dah

What do coats, pants, dresses, boots, suitcases, sleeping bags, and tent flaps have in common? They all use zippers. Have you ever wondered just how zippers work?

Zippers are made from two simple tools. One is a wedge; the other is a hook. These simple tools are among the oldest inventions that humans created. A wedge is an object with a slanted surface. If you push a wedge against an object, it pushes that object to the side. A hook is a curved piece of cloth or metal that grabs onto something else. Hooks and eyes are used on blouses and dresses. They are also used on some boots. In the old days, there were hooks on your shoes instead of holes and laces.

A zipper has a track with dozens of teeth and a slide. A slide is actually a group of wedges. The teeth are made of a hook and a hollow space. When you move the slide up the track, it forces the teeth together. The hollow spaces are filled. Your zipper is now zipped. When you pull the slide down, it forces the teeth apart. Your zipper is now unzipped.

The next time you zip up a jacket, think about how this little invention that's not even a hundred years old has helped to make your life just a little bit easier.

Cause and Effect

A cause makes something happen. The effect is what happens. When you read, notice cause-and-effect relationships. This will help you to understand how and why things occur.

This text will tell you how a roller coaster works. Look for the cause and effect.

1. Read the text. What causes a train to go up the first hill on a roller coaster?

   _____

   _____

2. What natural force causes the train to race down the first hill?

   _____

   _____

3. What is the effect (result) of the train reaching the bottom of the first hill?

   _____

   _____

Critical Thinking

How does the saying, "What goes up must come down" explain a cause-and-effect relationship?

_____

_____

_____

What Makes a Roller Coaster Roll?

What's your favorite ride at an amusement park? For many people, it's a roller coaster. No matter how high or how long, all roller coasters work in the same way. They depend on energy and gravity.

Some roller coaster cars look similar to the passenger cars on a train. But a roller coaster car has no engine or other source of power. The only help it gets is on the very first piece of track. That's when the car is pulled up the first hill, usually by a chain lift. After that, gravity takes over. The farther the car goes up, the farther it has to come down. As the car goes up, it collects energy. This energy gets used as the car zooms down the hill. That makes a new kind of energy. The new energy makes the car speed up the next hill.

The constant exchange of energy keeps the roller coaster going. That's why a roller coaster can go for hundreds of feet at high speeds. Some of the longest coasters have track that is a mile long! In time, though, the energy wears out. Then as the saying goes, "All good things must come to an end."

Draw Conclusions

When you draw conclusions, you make decisions based on what you read. The information is not stated in the story. You have to figure it out from what is provided. You may need to reread the story to decide the answers.

1. Read the text. What can you tell about Sonya's mom's personality?

   _____

   _____

2. Do you think that Sonya was the only child who did not have a father? Explain.

   _____

   _____

3. Do you think that the class enjoyed the Family and Me Dance? Explain.

   _____

   _____

Critical Thinking

Before the school changed its policy, was it fair to have a Daddy and Me Dance for daughters? Explain.

_____

_____

_____

The Dance

It was that time of year again—for the Daddy and Me Dance at school. Sonya could not stand the Daddy and Me Dance. She didn't have a daddy to take her, and Mrs. Ellsworth, her teacher, just didn't understand how Sonya felt. She'd look at Sonya, nod in that way she had that made Sonya feel unimportant, and suggest that Sonya bring an uncle. But Sonya and her mom didn't have anyone else. It was just the two of them. As Sonya walked home, she tried to figure out how to get out of even mentioning it to her mom this year.

When Sonya got home, though, her mother asked her to sit down because she had something to tell her. It turned out that Sonya's mom knew that the dance was coming up. She had called the school principal to complain that it wasn't fair to all of the children to make the dance specifically for girls and their dads. Although she was nice about it, she got her point across.

The night of the dance, Sonya went with her mom. Josh was there with his older cousin. Teresa was there with her aunt. Alicia, Tomas, and Juan were there with their uncles. Everyone had fun.

From then on, the dance was called the Family and Me Dance.

Draw Conclusions

When you draw conclusions, you make decisions based on what you read. The information is not stated in the story. You have to figure it out from what is provided. You may need to reread the story to decide the answers.

1. Read the text. What can you tell about Juan's personality?

   _____

   _____

2. Do you think that Juan was the only student in the class who had dreamed of exploring wonderful places? Explain.

   _____

   _____

3. Do you think that most of the class was surprised to find there are ice caves, hot springs, and a ghost town near Clarkville? Explain.

   _____

   _____

Critical Thinking

From the clue in the story, what can you conclude about Columbus, Magellan, and Lewis and Clark? Explain.

_____

_____

_____

I Want to Be an Explorer!

I have always wanted to be an explorer. Columbus, Magellan, Lewis and Clark, and the astronauts are my heroes. So, one day in third-grade class, we were telling what we wanted to do when we grew up. I said I wanted to be an explorer of strange and wonderful places. The other kids laughed. They told me there was nowhere left to explore.

Then my teacher said, "It's not true that Juan can't be an explorer. In fact," she said, "he may be able to go exploring this weekend!"

The class looked puzzled. One of the boys asked, "What would he explore? Where would he go?"

The teacher smiled and went to her bookcase. She took out a paperback book and showed the class its title: *Exploring Your World: How to Find Unexplored Places Right in Your Own Backyard.*

"Right in our own backyard?" some members of the class asked in disbelief. The teacher explained that "in your own backyard" meant places close to where you live. Then she opened the book and read, "There are ice caves, hot springs, and even an old ghost town not far from Clarkville."

"That's our town!" cried the class.

"I know," said the teacher and continued reading. "Take Howd Road west of town for eight miles to the dead end. There will be a gate with a *No Trespassing* sign. Go to the house nearby to get permission to pass. The owners will let you pass if you promise not to litter. Then follow the winding road for three miles until you come to a dry creek bed. The ice caves and the hot springs are a mile's hike up the mountain to your right. There is a sign and a footpath. The old ghost town is a short way down the other side of the mountain." She displayed the maps in the book.

"So you can be an explorer if you want," she concluded. "And you are never too young to start."

My class no longer thought it was foolish to want to be an explorer. In fact, quite a few of them decided to go exploring the next weekend!

Infer

When you infer, you make decisions based on information you read. The information is not given. You have to figure it out from the information provided. You may need to reread the story to decide the answers.

1. Read the story. In the beginning, the kingdom has no light. Why?

   _____

   _____

2. Is the palace big or small? How do you know?

   _____

   _____

3. Why can't Jackson open the cabinet door?

   _____

   _____

4. How do you think the light got locked inside the cabinet?

   _____

   _____

Critical Thinking

Could this story really happen? Explain why or why not.

_____

_____

_____

The Light Master

The kingdom had always been a dreary place. The sun did not shine. The king and queen's golden thrones did not glimmer, and their jewels did not sparkle. The kingdom had no light.

In the palace, Jackson did all of the cleaning. He huffed and puffed as he carried the bucket of sudsy water up and down the hundreds of castle stairs every day. Today, he would clean the highest tower and its filthy cabinet.

Jackson tugged and tugged at the cabinet door, but it would not budge. He twisted and turned its knob, but the door would not open. How could he clean the cabinet if its door would not open?

Jackson plopped down on the floor. He rested his back against the wall. To his surprise, the wall moved. He peeked behind it and saw a tiny case. When Jackson picked up the case, its lid flew open, and the wall slammed shut. To his shock, the case held a talking key that said, "Use me to unlock the light."

Jackson looked at the key and then at the cabinet. The key continued to shout, "Use me!" So Jackson turned the key, and the cabinet door sprang open. A small light fluttered out and began to grow. Soon the light filled the entire room. Suddenly, the sun shone brightly. The king and queen's golden thrones glimmered, and their jewels sparkled.

From that day on, the kingdom shimmered with light. The king and queen were so pleased that they made Jackson the kingdom's light master. It was the happiest day of his life!

Infer

When you infer, you make decisions based on information you read. The information is not given. You have to figure it out from the information provided. You may need to reread the story to decide the answers.

1. Read the story. Name the first three things that happened that let Kira know something odd is happening.

    _____

    _____

    _____

2. Why did Pete take Kira out for an ice cream breakfast?

    _____

    _____

3. Why did Kira's family have the party two days before her birthday?

    _____

    _____

Critical Thinking

Why did Kira's family act so strange on Saturday?

_____

_____

_____

One Strange Morning

When I woke up Saturday morning, I knew something was different. I couldn't hear my big brother, Pete, snoring in his room. Where was he anyway? I went to ask Mom, but I couldn't find her, either.

I went outside to see if the car was there, and it wasn't. I had been left home alone! That had never happened before. Then I saw my neighbor, Mrs. Huang, walking her dog. I asked her if she had seen my family. She mumbled something, scooped up her poodle, and hurried inside her house. Since she's usually friendly, this was strange.

It got even more weird when I saw the family car come around the corner, slow down, and then speed up and drive past my house! I started to run after it, but I saw Pete walking toward me. "Hey, Kira" he said, "let's go get, um, er, some ice cream." He grabbed my arm and led me to the corner shop. There, we ate huge ice cream sundaes for breakfast as if that was what we always did! By now I was pretty sure that aliens had taken over my family's bodies.

It was two days before my birthday. Yet when we got home, I saw that there was a giant "Happy Birthday!" sign on our garage. Inside were my parents, my grandparents, two of my closest friends, and even Mrs. Huang. And, there was a puppy! He was my special surprise. But the best part of the surprise party was finding out that aliens had not replaced my family.

Summarize

When you summarize, look for the main idea in the text. Identify what is most important and put it in your own words.

1. As you read the text, highlight only the important words or phrases. Then write four of them below.

   _____   _____

   _____   _____

2. Write three sentences that are NOT important in the text.

   _____

   _____

   _____

3. Sum up the main idea of the text in one sentence.

   _____

   _____

Critical Thinking

How did the italicized words in the text help you to figure out what should go in your summary?

_____

_____

_____

In the Rainforest

Imagine air that is thick with warmth and dampness. Birds chirp and monkeys chatter. Long, leafy vines twist around trees. Colorful flowers look up and try to see the sun. They peek through the branches of tall, green trees. What is this place? It is a rainforest.

Rainforests are like other forests in that they have many trees and plants. But rainforests are different in one special way. They are very wet. Most rainforests get a lot of rain. They are also warm most of the time. This keeps the trees and plants colorful and healthy. Rainforests like these are called *tropical rainforests*.

Other rainforests are wet, too, but for more reasons than rainfall. They also get a lot of water from fog and the moist air that comes from nearby oceans. Such rainforests are called *temperate rainforests*. They are not as warm as tropical rainforests.

Summarize

When you summarize, look for the main idea in the text. Identify what is most important and put it in your own words.

1. Read the text. Look for the answers to the following questions:

   Who? _____

   What? _____

   When? _____

   Where? _____

   Why? _____

   How? _____

2. Use the answers to the questions above to write four sentences that sum up the text.

   _____

   _____

   _____

   _____

Critical Thinking

How did identifying the answers to the question words help you to create a summary of the text?

_____

_____

_____

Ski Cross Craziness

A wild new sport was recently added to the Winter Olympics. It's called *ski cross*. Those who compete in it have to be brave—and maybe a little crazy, too!

Ski cross is a bit like motocross bike racing. But in ski cross, the racers are on skis. Four racers compete at once, whizzing on a downhill course full of twists and jumps. Ski cross racers can reach speeds of about 50 miles per hour (80.5 kph). That's amazingly fast! The skiers must be nimble and fearless to stay on their skis and out in front of the pack. Each one wants to be first to cross the finish line.

Ski cross racers are not allowed to pull or push one another. Even so, this is one tough sport. The skiers all start together and race in a group. They always jostle and bump as they struggle to pass one another. Sometimes they even knock into one another in midair as they go over jumps! Accidents happen, so the skiers must wear helmets to protect their heads.

The Winter Olympics have always had skiing events. But now, the Games include ski cross racing. This exciting new sport should make the Winter Olympics more fun than ever to watch.

Paraphrase

When you paraphrase, you restate the information in a text in your own words.

1. Read the text. Write one sentence to paraphrase what this text is about.

    _____

    _____

2. Explain the most common way that fossils are formed. Use the sequencing words to help you.

    First, _____

    Then, _____

    Next, _____

    Then, _____

    Finally, _____

Critical Thinking

How did summing up the text in your own words help you to understand what you read?

_____

_____

_____

Fun with Fossils

Have you ever found a rock that looks like a bone? Have you seen a rock with a plant print on it? These rocks are called *fossils*. They come from living things. After the plants and animals died, layers of soil covered them. The buried bones and teeth slowly turned into rock. This took millions of years.

Fossils tell us about the kinds of plants and animals that once lived on Earth. They are all that is left of living things from long ago. They may be leaf prints or footprints. They may be shell prints and skeleton prints. Fossils may even be made from an animal's waste!

There are many kinds of fossils, and they form in different ways. A fossil can form after a living thing is buried. It might be buried under mud or sand or ash from a volcano. A living thing may be frozen in ice. An animal may turn into a mummy if it is in a place with very dry air. Some fossils have been buried in tar for thousands of years.

How does a fossil form? First, an animal's body is buried by dirt. The soft parts of the body rot. Over time, minerals in the dirt seep into the bones. They make the bone hard and strong. This is the most common way that fossils form. Sometimes fossils may be made from a whole living thing. This happens when the animal is frozen or turned into a mummy. Then the soft parts are included, too.

Most fossils form near water. Nearby water, sand, and mud can bury the dead plant or animal. The mud piles up in layers, which turn into sedimentary rock. Fossils are often found in such rock.

Paraphrase

When you paraphrase, you restate the information in a text in your own words.

1. Read the text. Write one sentence to paraphrase each paragraph.

_____

_____

_____

_____

_____

2. Explain the way that a cavity forms. Use the sequencing words to help you.

First, _____

Then, _____

Next, _____

Finally, _____

Critical Thinking

How did summing up the text in your own words help you to understand what you read?

_____

_____

_____

Take Care of Your Teeth!

Have you ever had a cavity? If not, you're lucky. And if you've had one, you know it's not fun to get fixed. Let's look at what a cavity is, how you get one, and how you prevent it.

Your teeth are made up of four layers. Within the layers are the roots and nerves of a tooth. There's a kind of bacteria that's always in your mouth. When you eat foods full of sugar and starch, a reaction occurs. The bacteria change the sugar and starch into acid. Each time you eat these foods, the acid attacks your teeth for about 20 minutes. In time, the acid can work its way through a tooth, leaving a little hole. That hole is called a cavity. If you ignore it, the hole gets into the next layer of tooth. It can even get to the inside of your tooth. You'll know when this happens, because it hurts!

So how do you keep cavities from developing? Brush your teeth often, at least twice a day, for a full minute each time. Use floss to clear out the bits of food stuck between your teeth. Be sure to visit the dentist every six months to have your teeth cleaned. That's all you need!

Table of Contents

A table of contents appears at the start of a book. It shows the chapters that are in the book. By scanning the table of contents, you can tell if the book might answer a question you have.

1. Scan the table of contents. What is the name of the third chapter?

    _____

2. Read the table of contents. How many chapters are there in this book? (Note: The glossary and the index are not chapters.)

    _____

3. About how many pages are in this book? Explain.

    _____

    _____

4. In which chapter would you be most likely to read about the famous baseball player, Babe Ruth? Explain.

    _____

    _____

Critical Thinking

If you were writing a report on the legendary Sammy Sosa, would this book provide you with all of the information that you need? Explain.

_____

_____

_____

HISTORY OF BASEBALL

Table of Contents

Table of Contents

A table of contents appears at the start of a book. It shows the chapters that are in the book. By scanning the table of contents, you can tell if the book might answer a question you have.

1. Scan the table of contents. How many chapters are there in this book? (Note: The glossary and index are not chapters.)

   _____

2. Read the table of contents. About how many pages are in this book?

   _____

3. On what page would you most likely find the definition of a sweatshop?

   _____

4. In which chapter would you read about child labor?

   _____

5. Write the name(s) of the chapter(s) about unions.

   _____

Critical Thinking

If you were writing a report on the life of Henry Ford, an industrialist, would this book provide you with all of the information that you need? Explain.

   _____

   _____

   _____

The Industrial Revolution

Table of Contents

Index

An index is always on the last pages of a nonfiction book. It is an A-to-Z list of the important topics covered in the book. Specific words and ideas are given their own listings. If you want to see if a word or a person is mentioned in a book, use the index.

1. Scan the index. About how many pages are in this book? How do you know?

   _____

   _____

2. On what pages would you find information about the seed drill?

   _____

3. If you turned to page 22, what would you read about?

   _____

4. If you wanted to learn about the threshing machine, what page would you turn to?

   _____

Critical Thinking

Why is an index helpful in a nonfiction book?

_____

_____

_____

Inventions in the Food Industry

Index

Index

Skill Focus

> An index is always on the last pages of a nonfiction book. It is an A-to-Z list of the important topics covered in the book. Specific words and ideas are given their own listings. If you want to see if a word or a person is mentioned in a book, use the index.

1. Scan the index. How are the entries listed—in the order in which they appear in the book or in A-to-Z order? How do you know?

   _____

   _____

2. On what pages would you find information about the tongue?

   _____

3. If you turned to page 18, what would you read about?

   _____

4. If you wanted to learn about the part of the eye called the *iris*, what is the first page you would turn to?

   _____

Critical Thinking

Why isn't there an index in the back of a fiction book?

_____

_____

_____

The Five Senses

Index

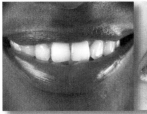  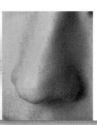  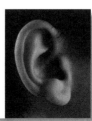

Glossary

A glossary is like a very short dictionary placed in the back of a nonfiction book. The glossary lists the definitions of important words used in the book. If you are reading and don't understand a word, turn to the glossary.

1. Scan the glossary. How are the entries listed—in the order in which they appear in the book or in A-to-Z order? How do you know?

   _____

   _____

2. Read the text. Use the word *toddler* in a sentence.

   _____

3. Draw a picture that shows the meaning of the word *infant*.

   [ ]

Critical Thinking

Think about the book's topic. Write one other word that could be included in this glossary.

_____

_____

_____

   © Shell Education

The Human Life Cycle

Glossary

ability—the quality of being able to do something

adolescence—the time of life between childhood and adulthood, usually thought of as the teenage years

adulthood—the time of life of a fully grown person

caregiver—person who takes care of another person

childhood—the state of being a child, usually thought of as between the ages of about 2 and 12

expression—the movement of the face to show different feelings, such as happiness, sadness, and anger

infancy—the beginning stage of human life; babyhood

infant—baby

life cycle—stages in the life of a living thing

mature—grow into adult level

moody—emotional, with a variety of changing feelings

primary—first or most important

responsibility—duty or obligation

social—able to get along well with others

toddler—young child of about one or two years old who, as a new walker, is a bit unsteady when walking and often falls

Glossary

A glossary is like a very short dictionary placed in the back of a nonfiction book. The glossary lists the definitions of important words used in the book. If you are reading and don't understand a word, turn to the glossary. You'll be glad you did.

1. Scan the glossary on the next page. You will see some words you don't know. List two below.

   _____   _____

2. Read the text. Write the definition of one of the words you listed above.

   _____

3. Use the word *carnivore* in a sentence.

   _____

4. Draw a picture that shows the meaning of the word *predator*.

   ┌───┐
   │   │
   │   │
   │   │
   │   │
   │   │
   └───┘

Critical Thinking

How does a glossary differ from an index?

   _____

   _____

   _____

Mammals

Glossary

carnivore—an animal that eats only meat

gestation—the amount of time a mammal spends developing inside its mother

habitat—the place where animals live in nature

herbivore—animals that eat only plants

hibernate—to spend the winter in a resting state

insulate—to keep warmth from escaping

limbs—the parts that stick out from an animal's body and are used to move or grasp

marsupial—a mammal that has a pouch in which to carry its young

monotreme—a mammal that lays eggs

offspring—the young of an animal or plant

omnivore—an animal that eats both plants and meat

predator—an animal that hunts, kills, and eats other animals

prey—any animal that is hunted by another

primate—a mammal that has hands instead of paws

rodent—a mammal with four limbs and sharp front teeth that do not stop growing

snout—long noses

vertebrate—an animals that has a spine (backbone)

Answer Key

Preview, p. 8

1. I think it will be about how things are made. I think so because it looks like it's going to have facts about clothing.
2. The names mentioned are Levi Strauss and Charles Macintosh.
3. Answers will vary; accept any two facts from the text.

Critical Thinking answers will vary. Sample: I can use the *Jeans* heading as a clue. I know the information about jeans is in the text under that heading.

Preview, p. 10

1. I think that the text will be about the International Space Station.
2. The two nations mentioned are the United States and the Soviet Union.
3. He wrote that it is like a city, and the author used that comparison because I have seen a city but I have never actually seen the Space Station. It helped me to know that it is huge and lots of people will live there.

Critical Thinking answers will vary. Sample: The events in the Space Station history section are listed in the order in which they occurred because that is the easiest to understand.

Predict, p. 12

1. It is a bat. I know because it only flies at night and makes noises to find insects.
2. It is a monkey. I know because of the long furry tail, chattering sounds, and people liking to watch the animals at the zoo.
3. It is a flying squirrel. Students will draw a picture of a squirrel jumping from tree to tree.

Critical Thinking answers will vary. Sample: Lito may be a writer when he grows up because he already likes to write. He may write for children or he may write brain teasers for adults.

Predict, p. 14

1. There will be a coyote and a scorpion in the story.
2. Answers will vary. Sample: The animals will probably have a problem because mammals don't make friends with insects that sting.
3. Answers will vary. Sample: Probably both animals would still be alive. OR The scorpion might have stung the coyote on land because he was angry that he wouldn't carry him across the stream.

Critical Thinking answers will vary. Sample: I was right about the animals that would be in the story and that they had a problem, but I was wrong about what the problem would be.

Prior Knowledge, p. 16

1. Answers will vary. Samples: Crayons come in many colors; Crayons are made of wax.
2. Answers will vary; accept any two facts from the text.
3. Answers will vary. Sample: What is the most popular crayon color? How many crayons are bought each year?

Critical Thinking answers will vary. Sample: I was able to picture crayons in my mind and think about what they look like and how to use them. The question about cooking oil and charcoal made me realize that the first crayons were really messy!

Prior Knowledge, p. 18

1. Answers will vary. Sample: I know that vampires drink blood and wear black capes.
2. Vampires sleep in coffins, and he is saying that windowless rooms are like coffins.
3. The vampire would probably like to see blood on the school lunch menu.

Critical Thinking answers will vary. Sample: I had to use what I knew about vampires to fill in the gaps so that the text made sense.

Answer Key *(cont.)*

Set a Purpose, p. 20

1. Answers will vary; student should write a question about panthers or other zoo animals.
2. Answers will vary; accept any two facts about panthers from the text.
3. Answers will vary; students must choose to add information about panthers, chimps, or reindeer. They can choose to add any kind of information not given in the text itself.

Critical Thinking answers will vary. Sample: No, but I can look it up online or in an encyclopedia or in a library book. OR Yes, it answered my question. (If the student's response to this is yes, make sure the text really did answer the question asked in #1.)

Set a Purpose, p. 22

1. Answers will vary. Sample: What is the most popular video game?
2. Answers will vary. Accept any two: Some games make you plan your moves; Action games develop your eye-hand coordination; Using your body in the game gives you exercise.
3. Answers will vary. Sample: I would write about a video game that helps me exercise while I play.

Critical Thinking answers will vary. Samples: It made me think about what I already know about video games. It helped me to know the text's topic in advance.

Ask Questions, p. 24

1. Answers will vary. Some students will know a lot about earthquakes (and may have lived through some); others will have almost no knowledge. Most students will realize that earthquakes are frightening events.
2. Answers will vary. Samples: Can an earthquake happen where I live? What happens during an earthquake? Can earthquakes be predicted? Can earthquakes be prevented?
3. Students should write the answers to the questions they posed. If the questions were not answered, help the student find the information.

Critical Thinking answers will vary. Samples: I can ask an adult to help me find the information. I can look it up online, in an encyclopedia, or in a library book.

Ask Questions, p. 26

1. Answers will vary; most students will have little knowledge about sea anemones. Some may make guesses about the clown fish in the photo, mistaking it for an anemone.
2. Answers will vary. Samples: Where can anemones be found?; How big are anemones?
3. Students should write the answers to the questions they posed. If the questions were not answered, help the student find the information.

Critical Thinking answers will vary. Samples: I can ask an adult to help me find the information. I can look it up online, in an encyclopedia, or in a library book.

Make Connections, p. 28

1. No, it is not a true story. I know because fish do not talk.
2. Answers will vary. Most students will want to believe they are most like Very Thoughtful as he is the hero of the story. It is important that the student explains his or her choice.
3. Answers will vary. Samples: I helped my sister learn to ride a bike; I helped my dad carry in the groceries.
4. Thoughtful and Thoughtless learned that it was too dangerous to live near fishermen, and it was safer to live in the wild.

Critical Thinking answers will vary but must include an example of a time when the student learned a difficult lesson. Sample: I got too close to the stove and burned my hand.

Make Connections, p. 30

1. Yes, it could happen in real life. I know because teachers like to help their students. The conversation sounds as if it really happened.
2. Answers will vary. Each student must briefly describe a time when he or she felt dumb.
3. Answers will vary. Sample: I know that I should answer the easier questions first, and then go back and work on the more difficult questions.
4. Answers will vary. Sample: I do not like taking tests because they are long and boring.

Critical Thinking answers will vary. Many students will realize that it would be hard to understand the text if one had never experienced taking a test.

Answer Key (cont.)

Context Clues, p. 32

1. The word *fortune* means "good luck." I know because the first line says "good luck" and the second line says that people around the world agree.
2. The word *shamrock* means "white clover." I know because the first sentence in the paragraph describes the plant and then it says, "you may know it as a shamrock."
3. The word *ancient* means "long ago." I know because the text says that the ancient priests lived long ago.

Critical Thinking answers will vary. Sample: Using context lets me read more difficult texts because I don't have to get stuck on tough words—I can use the sentences and words around the words I don't understand to figure out what they mean.

Context Clues, p. 34

1. The word *convenience* means "something suitable for performing with ease." I know this because the bird steals from a store that makes it easy for people to buy chips and other snacks.
2. The word *contents* means "the stuff inside the bag." I know this because the text says that lots of birds share the bag's contents.
3. The word *fantastic* means "great, really good, and wonderful." I know this because the manager says that the shoplifting bird is good for his business.

Critical Thinking answers will vary. Sample: Using context lets me read more difficult texts, because I can use the sentences and words around the words I don't understand to figure out what they mean.

Visualize, p. 36

1. Answers will vary. Samples: sandbox, magazine, bench
2. Students should draw Ben putting an earthworm in his mouth, Leah's shocked face, or Leah grabbing Ben and running home with him.
3. Answers will vary. Samples: worm, mother, eyes

Critical Thinking answers will vary. Sample: If the story later gives you information, you should change your mental image to match the description given.

Visualize, p. 38

1. Answers will vary. Samples: pink sky, space suits, red ground
2. Students should draw kids wearing spacesuits and helmets standing beneath a large solar blanket that looks like an awning on poles.
3. Answers will vary.

Critical Thinking answers will vary. Sample: I would like to go to a picnic on the moon. I would float around while I eat my food.

Story Elements, p. 40

1. Jamie, Mrs. Whitman
2. The story's setting is right now and it takes place in Jamie's kitchen and later on the basketball court.
3. The conflict is whether Jamie should visit his grandfather in the hospital or go play in an important basketball game.
4. The conflict is solved when Jamie's mom states that his grandfather would want him to play in the game with his team. Jamie plays the game, and his team wins.

Critical Thinking answers will vary. Samples: Yes, Jamie's grandpa will get better and watch Jamie's playoff game. OR No, Jamie's grandpa will still be in the hospital and miss the playoff game.

Story Elements, p. 42

1. The story takes place in the attic. I think that the setting is long ago, because the family seems quite big, the kids all sleep in the cold attic, and Hannah is a child going to work.
2. The conflict in this story is that Hannah is worried about her first day at work.
3. The conflict is not worked out. It will probably be solved in the next few pages when the writer tells us about what happens during Hannah's first day at the boarding house.

Critical Thinking answers will vary. Samples: Yes, Hannah will do a good job on her first day of work because she is concerned about doing a good job. OR No, everything will go wrong on Hannah's first day, and she will be fired or feel discouraged because that would make the story more interesting.

Answer Key *(cont.)*

Plot, p. 44

1. Tim's problem in the beginning is that he wants to learn to skateboard, but he doesn't have a skateboard.
2. Matt is Tim's older brother. He won't share his skateboard with Tim because it took Matt so long to earn the money to buy it.
3. Tim is feeling discouraged because he knows he's too little to mow lawns to earn money, so he doesn't know when or if he'll ever have enough money to buy a skateboard.
4. He will earn money for the skateboard by walking the neighbor's dog, Tutu.

Critical Thinking answers will vary. Sample: No, most stories are longer so their plots are more involved and are not solved as quickly.

Plot, p. 46

1. Principal Pallen, Detective Dana, Lance Larkin
2. Lance Larkin does not appear in the story.
3. The problem in this story is that someone has stolen a trophy from the school, and Detective Dana is working to find out who is the thief.
4. No, the problem is not solved. They do not know the name of the thief. They only know that Lance Larkin is not the thief.

Critical Thinking answers will vary. Sample: No, this is not the end of the story because the crime has not been solved. This appears to be a middle part of the whole story.

Characters, p. 48

1. Benjamin, Shane, and their mother
2. Shane is Benjamin's brother; the other person is Benjamin's mother.
3. Answers will vary. Sample: Shane is probably the younger brother because he sleeps in the lower bunk. He does not yell at Benjamin when he starts playing his horn, so he is probably not a fighter. He snores.

Critical Thinking answers will vary. Sample: I would add a sister for Benjamin. She would actually complain about the horn playing, but he would ignore her.

Characters, p. 50

1. Fox and Bear
2. Answers will vary. Sample: Bear was not too smart and tried too hard to cooperate with the wicked Fox.
3. The Fox was jealous and played a mean joke on Bear that made him lose his tail.
4. Answers will vary. Sample: Bear learned not to be so trusting because of this bad experience.

Critical Thinking answers will vary. Sample: I would rather have Bear as a friend because he wasn't wicked. OR I would rather have Fox as a friend because he was clever.

Title and Headings, p. 52

1. This text will be about finding out about news long ago and today.
2. News Then: Accept any one fact from the text; Newspapers were small; They had very little news; They were printed once a week; Few people could read, so many shared one newspaper. News Now: Accept any one fact from the text; People read the news on the Internet via their computer or cell phones; Some people watch TV news; People listen to the radio news in their cars; Most newspapers are printed daily, and many people read them.

Critical Thinking answers will vary. Sample: The writer used headings to divide the text into sections so it was easy to know which part was about the past and which part was about today.

Answer Key *(cont.)*

Title and Headings, p. 54

1. The three kinds of measurements are length, distance, and volume.
2. People once used their own body parts to help measure the length of things.
3. Draw a line to match each heading with its main idea.

Heading	Main Idea
Measuring Length	The Romans were the first to measure a mile.
Measuring Distance	People once used seeds to find out the volume of a container.
Measuring Volume	Hands, feet, and other body parts were used to determine how long something was.

Critical Thinking answers will vary. Sample: Yes, it explained why it is important for everyone to agree on the same measurements. OR No, it didn't make it clear why we still need to make accurate measurements.

Typeface and Captions, p. 56

1. The special typeface is boldface.
2. The words *colonial times* are in boldface.
3. Answers will vary. Sample: A family works together to harvest wheat.

Critical Thinking answers will vary. Sample: It might mean that the people in colonial times were not so different from people today because families also took care of each other back then.

Typeface and Captions, p. 58

1. Answers will vary. Sample: It means that the text will tell about how and when bikes were invented.
2. The special typeface is italic.
3. The words in italics are *velocipede* and *penny-farthing*.
4. The pictures and captions helped me to picture the bikes in my mind because I've never seen these old-fashioned bicylces.

Critical Thinking answers will vary. Sample: My mom rides her tricycle around our neighborhood.

Graphics, p. 60

1. The picture looks like a satellite (students may also guess spacecraft).
2. There are stars in the box.
3. five
   Wolf 359 is the star that is farthest from Earth.
   Barnard's Star is 35 trillion miles from Earth.

Critical Thinking answers will vary. Sample: The object in the picture is manmade. I know this because this item is not naturally found in the universe, so it has to be made.

Graphics, p. 62

1. The organs of the human body in the chest and neck area are shown in the large picture.
2. The inset is a close-up view of the inside of the lungs.
3. The diaphragm is below the heart; The liver is behind the lungs; The trachea is outside the lungs.

Critical Thinking answers will vary. Sample: The diagram shows what the text talks about so I don't have to try to picture it. It would be hard to picture lungs, because I've never seen them in real life.

Topic Sentences, p. 64

1. The Caribbean Sea is a pretty place.
2. The Caribbean Sea is actually a part of the Atlantic Ocean.
3. Answers will vary. Sample: Because of long-ago wars, some of the Caribbean islands belong to other countries, while some of them are independent nations.

Critical Thinking answers will vary. Sample: The next time I read a nonfiction text, I will look for topic sentences to help me understand the text.

Topic Sentences, p. 66

1. You can use things up instead of wasting them.
2. You do not always need to have new things.
3. By being responsible consumers, we help our environment.

   This topic sentence is at the end of the paragraph because it is summing up the whole text.

Critical Thinking answers will vary. Sample: The next time I read a nonfiction text, I will be aware of topic sentences and keep an eye out for them. They are like signs that guide me through the text.

Main Idea, p. 68

1. The main idea is that the seahorse is a very strange kind of fish.
2. Detail: (accept one) It has a head shaped like a horse's head; It can be tiny or large; It likes to live in warm water, hardly ever swims.

   Detail: (accept one) A seahorse's tail is like a monkey's; It holds on to sea plants with its tail; It eats shrimp and baby fish.

   Detail: (accept one) The seahorse dad gives birth to the babies; He has about 100 at a time.

Critical Thinking answers will vary. Sample: Scanning the text first helped me to know what the text would be about so I could find the main idea quickly.

Main Idea, p. 70

1. The main idea is that the octopus is an awesome sea creature.
2. Answers will vary. Accept any four details from the text: There are 50 kinds; They can be tiny or large; Big ones can drag human adults to the bottom of the sea; They have eight arms with rows of suckers; If they lose an arm, it grows back; They move around on the ends of their arms; They have no bones; They change color; They spray purple ink to confuse predators.

Critical Thinking answers will vary. Sample: Scanning the text for topic sentences and knowing that one of them was going to be the main idea made it simple to find the main idea of the text.

Details, p. 72

1. Main Idea: Nell and Chan can make themselves tiny and move through cyberspace to fix virus problems in computers.
2. Details: Nell whirls around to become tiny; She travels through her mouse; Chan gets small and goes with her through cyberspace; They land in the hard drive of a computer; They put on anti-virus fighting gear and get to work.

Critical Thinking answers will vary. Sample: The details in a fictional story may be things that could never happen (like people shrinking and traveling through cyberspace), while the details in a nonfiction text will be facts.

Details, p. 74

2. Main Idea: There are sites on the Internet that can help you do your homework.

   Details: There are websites for all subjects; Some websites have animated videos about a topic; Some websites have a way for you to email a real person and get an email answer; Some websites have resources for projects.

Critical Thinking answers will vary. Sample: The details in a fictional story may be things that could never happen, while the details in a nonfiction text will be facts.

Main Idea and Details, p. 76

1. Answers will vary, but accept any fad mentioned in the text.
2. Main idea: A fad is something that suddenly everyone wants to have or do. Answers will vary. Sample: Details: It can be something you want to own (like a toy, a video game, or a pet rock); It can be a hairstyle (feathered, big hair); It can be something you wear (clothes, jewelry).

Critical Thinking answers will vary. Sample: I had to think about which were the major details of all the little details given. I only included the major ones.

Answer Key (cont.)

Time Order, p. 78

1. 4, 2, 3, 1
2. Answers will vary. Sample: The writer will throw seaweed at Corey and Grandpa.
3. Answers will vary. Sample: It was good that this story was told in chronological order because telling events in the order in which they happened makes the most sense for a diary entry.

Critical Thinking answers will vary. Sample: Yes, because people who keep diaries just write the highlights of what happened. OR No, the group probably had some more adventures on the beach that the writer will tell about.

Time Order, p. 80

1. 4, 5, 2, 1, 3
2. 1849: Gold miners arrived; 1881: Borax miners arrived; 1920s: Scotty's Castle was built; 1933: became a national monument

Critical Thinking answers will vary. Sample: Authors put things in chronological order because if things were told out of order, the reader could get confused.

Logical Order, p. 82

2. Patty's plans: She would sell the milk; She would use the money to buy chickens; She would sell the chickens' eggs to the baker's wife; She would use the money to get a beautiful dress and a fancy hat; All the young men would talk to her; Polly Shaw would be jealous of her.

Critical Thinking answers will vary. Sample: Patty's mother meant that you should not act as if something will definitely happen because something might go wrong to mess up your plans.

Logical Order, p. 84

1. Answers will vary. Sample: My ice cream sundae had ice cream, syrup, sprinkles, chopped candy pieces, and whipped cream.
2. 1. Get out all the ingredients plus a bowl and a spoon; 2. Put a scoop of your favorite ice cream into the bowl; 3. Pour sauce onto top; if it needs to be heated, get an adult's help; 4. Add the nuts; 5. Add whipped cream; 6. Put a maraschino cherry on top; 7. Enjoy and clean up after yourself.

Critical Thinking answers will vary. Sample: You would make it before you actually make the ice cream sundae. That means it would go before the first step.

Fact and Opinion, p. 86

1. Answers will vary; accept any fact from the letter.
2. Answers will vary; accept any opinion from the letter.
3. F, F, O, F, O

Critical Thinking answers will vary. Sample: Ronin's opinion about grandparents living with grandkids is that it is a lot of fun.

Fact and Opinion, p. 88

1. Answers will vary; accept any fact from the text.
2. Answers will vary; accept any opinion from the text.
3. O, F, F, O, F

Critical Thinking answers will vary. Sample: The writer says lots of positive things about sugar maples, so the writer wants the reader to agree.

Proposition and Support, p. 90

1. Answers will vary. Sample: I think the proposition will be that children should or should not wear pajamas in school.
2. The writer's proposition is that students should wear pajamas to school.
3. Answers will vary; accept any three of the following: Wearing pajamas lets students feel warm, comfortable, and safe; Students who feel warm, comfortable, and safe will do better in school; Fewer students will miss the bus if they don't have to get dressed; School would be more fun; People would like wearing their pajamas and having hot chocolate during story time.

Critical Thinking answers will vary. Samples: Yes, the writer made good points about why kids would do better in school if they wore pajamas. OR No, the writer did not persuade me to believe that students should wear pajamas because I think that students wouldn't pay attention to their schoolwork.

Answer Key (cont.)

Proposition and Support, p. 92

1. I think the proposition will be that people should eat right.
2. The writer's proposition is that it is important to eat right to be healthy.
3. Accept any three of the following: Eating right means eating healthy food; Eat fruits and vegetables instead of cookies and candy; Fruits and vegetables contain lots of vitamins and minerals; Bread, nuts, and milk are good sources of protein and build muscles and bones.

Critical Thinking answers will vary. Sample: Proposition and support makes a statement and then gives reasons why the reader should believe it. It is like problem and solution because it identifies a problem (eating unhealthy foods) and the solution (choosing healthy foods to eat).

Author's Purpose, p. 94

1. The author wrote this text to tell the reader about air shows.
2. The author likes air shows. I know because of the title, which says that air shows are fun. Also, the author seems to know a lot about old planes.
3. It sounds like the author might disapprove of the dangerous tricks in which people stood on planes and were held in place only by straps on their feet.

Critical Thinking answers will vary. Sample: I think the author would say that an air show doesn't last very long, and people can stand the noise for such a short period of time. It's obvious that the author is in favor of air shows even though they can be noisy.

Author's Purpose, p. 96

1. The author wrote this text to promote having school four days a week instead of five.
2. The author feels that it is really important for kids to have time to relax.
3. The author would want kids to sleep late.

Critical Thinking answers will vary. Sample: The author would disagree and say that it is too much to ask kids to go to school six days a week and that kids' lives are already too hectic going to school five days a week.

Compare and Contrast, p. 98

1.

Kangaroo	Rabbit
Ears: stand straight up	Ears: stand straight up
Legs: strong back legs, tiny front legs; hop only on back legs	Legs: strong back legs, hop on all fours
Where they live: Australia	Where they live: all around the world
Babies: called joeys; stay in mother's front pouch	Babies: called kits; born in underground nests
Size: mostly large, up to six feet tall and 100 pounds	Size: mostly small, less than two feet long and weigh under five pounds
Color: brown, red, or gray fur	Color: brown and gray fur
Tail: long, strong	Tail: short, fluffy

2. Students should draw a kangaroo and a rabbit side by side.

Critical Thinking answers will vary but should be supported by facts. Samples: I think they are more alike because they are both mammals, give birth to live young, move around by hopping, may have similar color fur. OR I think they are more different because their size is nowhere near the same, kangaroos only live on one continent, kangaroos have forelegs that look like arms.

Answer Key (cont.)

Compare and Contrast, p. 100

1.

Sarcosuchus of Long Ago	Crocodile of Today
Head: long head with sharp teeth	Head: long head with sharp teeth
Skin: tough, thick scales	Skin: tough, thick scales
Tail: strong, used for swimming	Tail: strong, used for swimming
Size: about 50 feet long	Size: about 16 feet long
Prey: other dinosaurs	Prey: deer and water buffalo

2. Students should draw two identical crocodiles with one about three times bigger than the other. The larger one must be labeled *Sarcosuchus*, and the smaller one must be labeled *Crocodile*.

Critical Thinking answers will vary. Sample: *Sarcosuchus* and a modern crocodile are more alike than different because the main differences are their size and the size of their prey.

Classify, p. 102

1.

10-Speed Bikes	BMX Bike	Tandem Bikes
racing on roads for a long distance	competing in a dirt bike race doing tricks on ramps	riding at a beach riding with a friend

Critical Thinking answers will vary. Sample: I could probably use any kind of bike to ride to a friend's house.

Classify, p. 104

1. I think the text will be about groups of fierce dinosaurs, probably divided by size.
2. Answers will vary. Possible titles: Fierce Dinosaurs; Dinosaur Predators; Dinosaurs That Ate Other Dinosaurs. One box should be labeled *Small Predators* or *Small Meat Eaters*; inside that box should be *velociraptor* and *ceratosaurus*. One box should be labeled *Big Predators* or *Big Meat Eaters*; Inside that box should be *tyrannosaurus* and *giganotosaurus*.

Critical Thinking answers will vary. Sample: Listing the information in categories helped me to understand what I read. I had to think about which group each dinosaur mentioned belonged in.

Cause and Effect, p. 106

1. Moving the zipper's slide makes the zipper's teeth push together.
2. When you pull a zipper slide down, it forces the teeth apart and undoes the zipper.
3. Answers will vary. Sample: Before zippers were invented, people fastened things using buttons and snaps.

Critical Thinking answers will vary. Sample: Zippers are easier to use or cheaper than other kinds of fasteners.

Cause and Effect, p. 108

1. Usually a chain lift pulls a train up the first hill on a roller coaster.
2. Gravity is the natural force that causes the train to race down the first hill.
3. The effect of the train reaching the bottom of the first hill is that is has enough energy to carry it up the next hill.

Critical Thinking answers will vary. Sample: The saying means that gravity is always at work, so the force of gravity will eventually pull down anything that goes up.

Answer Key *(cont.)*

Draw Conclusions, p. 110

1. Answers will vary. Sample: I can tell that Sonya's mom's personality is strong but kind. She stands up for Sonya with the school principal in a polite way.
2. No, Sonya was not the only child who did not have a father. At the end of the story, five other kids are there with people other than fathers.
3. Yes, I think they enjoyed it because it says that everyone had fun.

Critical Thinking answers will vary. Sample: No, it was not fair to have a Daddy and Me Dance for daughters because it excluded the boys and embarrassed the daughters who didn't have fathers.

Draw Conclusions, p. 112

1. Answers will vary. Sample: Juan wants to be an explorer. He's curious and wants to see new places.
2. Answers will vary. Sample: I doubt that Juan was the only child in the class who had dreamed of exploring wonderful places. Many kids want to be explorers, and that was shown to be true at the end of the story when so many of them got excited about the nearby places they could explore.
3. Answers will vary. Sample: Yes, the class members acted surprised that there were ice caves, hot springs, and a ghost town near their town of Clarkville because they cried out, "That's our town!"

Critical Thinking answers will vary. Sample: I can conclude that Columbus, Magellan, and Lewis and Clark were all explorers because Juan says he wants to be an explorer and then lists these names as people who are his "heroes."

Infer, p. 114

1. In the beginning, the kingdom has no light because all the light is trapped inside a cabinet.
2. The palace is big. I know because there are hundreds of castle stairs.
3. Jackson can't open the cabinet door because it is locked, and the key is hidden in a box behind a moving wall.
4. Answers will vary. Sample: A wicked witch put a curse on the castle by trapping the light inside the cabinet.

Critical Thinking sample answer: No, this story could not really happen because there is no way to trap all of the light inside a cabinet.

Infer, p. 116

1. Her brother and mother are missing; Kira had been left home completely alone; Mrs. Huang, who is usually friendly, goes in her house.
2. Pete took Kira out for an ice cream breakfast because he was trying to give his parents time to set up the surprise party.
3. Answers will vary. Sample: Kira's family had the surprise party two days before her birthday because it is easier to surprise someone when it's not his or her actual birthday.

Critical Thinking sample answer: They were trying to keep the party and the puppy a secret until the surprise party was all set up for Kira.

Summarize, p. 118

1. Answers will vary. Sample: warmth, dampness, birds, monkeys
2. Answers will vary. Sample: Colorful flowers look up and try to see the sun; Birds chirp and monkeys chatter; This keeps the trees and plants are colorful and healthy.
3. Both tropical and temperate rainforests have a lot of moisture, plants, trees, and animal life.

Critical Thinking sample answer: The italicized words were the names of the two types of rainforests. This let me know that both kinds of rainforests should be in my summary.

Answer Key *(cont.)*

Summarize, p. 120

1. Who: ski cross racers; What: a sport called *ski cross*; When: added recently to the Winter Olympics; Where: on a downhill course; Why: to see who will be the first to cross the finish line; How: four racers go down a course full of twists and jumps and often bang into each other.

2. Answers will vary. Sample: Ski cross is a new sport recently added to the Winter Olympics. Groups of four ski cross racers speed down a course with twists and jumps. It is dangerous because the racers are going so fast and often bang into one another. They have to wear helmets to protect their heads.

Critical Thinking answers will vary. Sample: Identifying the answers to the question words helped me to create a summary of the text because it let me know what things were important and should be included.

Paraphrase, p. 122

1. Answers will vary. Sample: Fossils are the remains of plants or animals that have become part of rock.

2. Answers will vary. Sample: First, an animal's body gets buried in dirt; Then, the soft parts rot; Next, minerals seep into the bones; Then, the bones harden into rock; Finally, the bones become a fossil.

Critical Thinking answers will vary. Sample: Summing up the text in my own words helped me to understand what I read because I had to think about how a fossil forms.

Paraphrase, p. 124

1. Answers will vary. Sample: A cavity is not fun to get fixed. The bacteria in your mouth creates an acid that attacks your teeth and can cause a cavity. You should brush and floss your teeth and visit the dentist every six months to prevent cavities.

2. Answers will vary. Sample: First, you eat food; Then, the bacteria in your mouth change the sugar and starch in the food into acid; Next, this acid attacks your teeth; Finally, the acid works its way through your tooth, leaving a small hole.

Critical Thinking answers will vary. Sample: Summing up the text in my own words helped me to understand what I read and made me think about how a cavity forms.

Table of Contents, p. 126

1. "Dressed to Play Ball"

2. 8

3. There are about 28 pages in the book because the index begins on page 28.

4. I would most likely read about Babe Ruth in "Baseball Greats" because he was one of the best players of all time.

Critical Thinking answers will vary. Sample: This book would not give all of the information needed to write a report about Sammy Sosa because it is an overview about baseball and not an in-depth work on players.

Table of Contents, p. 128

1. 13 chapters

2. There are about 31 pages in the book.

3. page 16

4. "The Laboring Child"

5. "Labor Unions Get Their Start" and "Troubled Times for Unions"

Critical Thinking answers will vary. Sample: If I were writing a report on the life of Henry Ford, this book would not have all of the information I need because it is an overview of the Industrial Revolution. I would need in-depth information about Ford that I could get from a biography.

Answer Key *(cont.)*

Index, p. 130

1. There are about 26 pages in the book. I know because there are no page numbers higher than that in the index.
2. pages 5, 24, and 25
3. If I turned to page 22, I would read about restaurants and cast-iron stoves.
4. page 5

Critical Thinking answers will vary. Sample: An index is helpful in a nonfiction book because it helps you search through all of the topics, definitions, and descriptions in the book.

Index, p. 132

1. The entries are listed in order from A to Z. I can tell this by looking at the first letters of the words.
2. pages 22–23
3. If I turned to page 18, I would read about the nose.
4. If I wanted to learn about the part of the eye called the *iris*, I would turn to page 10.

Critical Thinking answers will vary. Sample: There is no index in the back of a fiction book because there are no important concepts defined and described in a story.

Glossary, p. 134

1. They are listed in order from A to Z. I can tell it is in this order by looking at the first few letters of each word.
2. Answers will vary. Sample: The toddler took three steps and fell down.
3. Pictures will vary. Students must draw a human infant.

Critical Thinking answers will vary. Samples: adolescent, teenager, child, elderly, senior citizen

Glossary, p. 136

1. Answers will vary. Accept any two words from the glossary list.
2. Answers will vary. Make sure the student writes the definition for one of the words listed above.
3. Answers will vary. Sample: A tiger is a carnivore because it eats other animals.
4. Pictures will vary. Students must draw a predator hunting another animal.

Critical Thinking answers will vary. Sample: A glossary gives the definitions of important words in a book. An index tells the pages on which important words and concepts in a nonfiction book.

Contents of the Teacher Resource CD

Skill	Filename		Skill	Filename
Preview			**Story Elements**	
In Your Closet	page008.pdf page009.pdf		*For Grandpa*	page040.pdf page041.pdf
The International Space Station	page010.pdf page011.pdf		*The Key*	page042.pdf page043.pdf
Predict			**Plot**	
Guess What It Is	page012.pdf page013.pdf		*The Skateboard*	page044.pdf page045.pdf
Coyote and the Scorpion	page014.pdf page015.pdf		*A Suspect Is Cleared*	page046.pdf page047.pdf
Prior Knowledge			**Characters**	
Colorful Crayons	page016.pdf page017.pdf		*Bothersome Benjamin*	page048.pdf page049.pdf
Interview with the Springside School Vampire	page018.pdf page019.pdf		*Why Bear Has No Tail: An American Indian Legend*	page050.pdf page051.pdf
Set a Purpose			**Title and Headings**	
A Visit to the Zoo	page020.pdf page021.pdf		*Getting the News: Then and Now*	page052.pdf page053.pdf
Games Worth Playing	page022.pdf page023.pdf		*Why Measure?*	page054.pdf page055.pdf
Ask Questions			**Typeface and Captions**	
Earthquake!	page024.pdf page025.pdf		*Not So Different*	page056.pdf page057.pdf
The Anemone	page026.pdf page027.pdf		*Bike Beginnings*	page058.pdf page059.pdf
Make Connections			**Graphics**	
The Three Fishes	page028.pdf page029.pdf		*Outer Space*	page060.pdf page061.pdf
The Girl Who Thought She Was Dumb	page030.pdf page031.pdf		*Your Lungs and How They Work*	page062.pdf page063.pdf
Context Clues			**Topic Sentences**	
You're in Luck!	page032.pdf page033.pdf		*The Caribbean Sea*	page064.pdf page065.pdf
Feathered Thief Boosts Business	page034.pdf page035.pdf		*Be a Responsible Consumer!*	page066.pdf page067.pdf
Visualize			**Main Idea**	
Watching Ben	page036.pdf page037.pdf		*Seahorses*	page068.pdf page069.pdf
A Picnic on Mars	page038.pdf page039.pdf		*The Octopus*	page070.pdf page071.pdf

Contents of the Teacher Resource CD (cont.)

Skill	Filename
Details	
Cyber Kids to the Rescue	page072.pdf page073.pdf
Help Is Just a Click Away	page074.pdf page075.pdf
Main Idea and Details	
Fad-tastic Fads	page076.pdf page077.pdf
Time Order	
Seaweed Scare	page078.pdf page079.pdf
Death Valley	page080.pdf page081.pdf
Logical Order	
Patty the Milkmaid	page082.pdf page083.pdf
How to Make an Ice Cream Sundae	page084.pdf page085.pdf
Fact and Opinion	
Letter to My Pen Pal	page086.pdf page087.pdf
The Sugar Maple Tree	page088.pdf page089.pdf
Proposition and Support	
Pajamas Belong at School	page090.pdf page091.pdf
Eating Right	page092.pdf page093.pdf
Author's Purpose	
Exciting Air Shows	page094.pdf page095.pdf
Wanted: Relaxation	page096.pdf page097.pdf
Compare and Contrast	
What Goes Hop, Hop, Hop?	page098.pdf page099.pdf
One Big Croc	page100.pdf page101.pdf
Classify	
Bikes, Bikes, Bikes	page102.pdf page103.pdf
Dino Predators Big and Small	page104.pdf page105.pdf

Skill	Filename
Cause and Effect	
Zippety Doo Dah	page106.pdf page107.pdf
What Makes a Roller Coaster Roll?	page108.pdf page109.pdf
Draw Conclusions	
The Dance	page110.pdf page111.pdf
I Want to Be an Explorer!	page112.pdf page113.pdf
Infer	
The Light Master	page114.pdf page115.pdf
One Strange Morning	page116.pdf page117.pdf
Summarize	
In the Rainforest	page118.pdf page119.pdf
Ski Cross Craziness	page120.pdf page121.pdf
Paraphrase	
Fun with Fossils	page122.pdf page123.pdf
Take Care of Your Teeth!	page124.pdf page125.pdf
Table of Contents	
History of Baseball	page126.pdf page127.pdf
The Industrial Revolution	page128.pdf page129.pdf
Index	
Inventions in the Food Industry	page130.pdf page131.pdf
The Five Senses	page132.pdf page133.pdf
Glossary	
The Human Life Cycle	page134.pdf page135.pdf
Mammals	page136.pdf page137.pdf

Notes

© Shell Education